HIGHER PURSUITS

Positioning Yourself for Everyday Revival

SARAH FRANCIS MARTIN

Higher Pursuits: Positioning Yourself For Everyday Revival

Copyright 2022 by Sarah Francis Martin

All Rights Reserved. No part of Book Title may be reproduced, stored in a retrieval system, or transmitted, in any form or by any means—by electronic, mechanical, photocopying, recording or otherwise—in any form without permission. Thank you for buying an authorized edition of this book and for complying with copyright laws.

BIBLE REFERENCE COPYRIGHTS (if applicable)

**Must be included for all versions referenced in the manuscript. See this Bible Version Guide for most common Scripture copyrights.

Scripture taken from the English Standard Version Bible, ESV®, Copyright © 2007, 2011, 2016 by Crossway, a publishing ministry of Good News Publishers. Used by permission.

Scripture taken from The Voice, VOICE®, Copyright © 2008, 20011, Thomas Nelson. Used by permission.

Cover Design: Allan Nygren

Interior Design: Allan Nygren

Paperback ISBN: 978-0-578-32083-0

First Edition

Printed in the United States.

For Hailey and Hannah: The girls who do this Higher Pursuits thing every day. You inspire me and call me higher.

WHAT GALS LIKE YOU HAD TO SAY

These women are just like you with their range of ages, locations, and life stages. Here is their experience of reading Higher Pursuits:

While reading Higher Pursuits, the Lord stirred in me to erase the desire for what used to be and instead press on towards what God has for me right here and now. It convicted me to take inventory of my spiritual disciplines and make them a priority because the world we are living in wants to confuse us of what is truth. This book draws you to the Word of God to find truth and encourages us to posture ourselves in a desire for revival and not fear.

Emma Koch

While reading Higher Pursuits, I sensed God pulling my chair forward, garnering my whole attention and showing me gently where I have been settling for lesser things. This book is not only a guide for someone learning how to follow God for the first time, but a guide for the weary saint to rekindle that relationship with their first love. This is not just a book about revival, this is a book about discipleship. It's riveting. It's pointed. It's so needed at this hour.

Jamie Stapleton

While reading Higher Pursuits, I felt like I was sitting on a cozy couch in my living room with my best friends discussing how we can take our spiritual lives to another level. I felt like a hand was being reached out to me calling me two leave the lesser lovers (earthly distractions and things pulling on my affections) and go after my greatest calling; intimacy with God.

Sheena Musembi

While reading Higher Pursuits, the Lord stirred in me the excitement that women are awakening everywhere in this hour to the call to go deeper! If you're not satisfied with status quo Christianity, if you know there is more, and if you desire to live in complete surrender and abandonment to Jesus…. this book is for you! It put into words the deep longings of my heart and equipped me with practical steps in order to keep pursuing this laid down life!

Misti Mott

While reading Higher Pursuits, the Lord stirred in me the desire to revisit former definitions of what revival looks like. Often it brings up images of carefully curated programs, pitched tents, fast and loud church services, music to elicit a specific emotion but often void of actual revival. Sarah reminded me of what everyday revival and discipleship looks like in real time! I'm excited to live it out loud!

Sethlina Amakye

While reading Higher Pursuits, the Lord stirred in me a desire to hold fast to his promise that his presence really is for me all the days of my life. There are no, if, and's, but's, or maybes. If I choose to seek him, he will come and I can receive the gift of a life marked by his glory, love, and everyday revival. I am convinced that those burning for a moment with him will always be met with more of His presence, character, and love. I am convicted and uplifted that turning to Jesus in the small moments of my day when I am tempted to turn to lesser things can impact my life, the lives of those around me, and eternity if I choose to press into his presence and the higher pursuits of his beloved ones. Hannah Smith Reading Higher Pursuits helped me break down those walls that I need to be some great biblical scholar to go deeper with God. I'm learning that He just wants to meet me where I am-- a normal gal trying to be a working mom, wife, and lover of Jesus. This book has helped me shift out all the distractions, chaos, and noise that is swirling around us these days and dive into relationship with my Creator. Because that's what we really need and desire--to KNOW Him and be KNOWN by Him.

Mallory Neill

After the past two years, it is easy to find ourselves feeling discouraged. Sarah's words bring hope and excitement for a weary soul. Her words of revival and desiring more of the Holy Spirit stirred in me an expectancy for true revival. Her writing is beautiful, and this book is thought-provoking, yet filled with practical prompts which help guide to a deeper connection with the Holy Spirit.

Kristin Wall

The temporal versus the eternal is the major theme of our Bible or the world without Christ versus eternal life beginning now with him with the indwelling Holy Spirit. As I read Higher Pursuits, I was encouraged to lean into Scripture such as Luke 11:11-13 where Jesus states that we can have more of the Holy Spirit if we ask. Sarah identifies these temporal snares that hinder us from having a full experience of all that God is and what I can have in Him. My focus now is to identify and discard the lesser things in my life. I am encouraged to move forward to a deeper season with my Father and my Savior.

Susie Wright

In Higher Pursuits, Sarah teaches us how to silence the noise of the world and shift our focus to Kingdom, revival, and heavenly ways in a realistic and accessible way. Reading through this book you will not only feel like you're talking to your friend about the things that truly matter but also learn how to dig into the word and draw closer to God no matter where you are on your faith journey.

Kacey Randolph

Excitement began to rise in my spirit even as I began reading even the introduction. I KNEW I was in the right place for I've been praying for revival the past two years. Higher Pursuits challenged me to go deeper in personal revival. To push past my own insecurities. To be real and raw with God. To embrace spiritual discipline. To wrestle with the truths of scripture. To surrender and draw near to God every day so that His Spirit will empower me to carry His light with bold confidence into this dark world.

Teresa Duggins

Through Higher Pursuits, the concept of revival shifts from complicated and unattainable to everyday encounters with the Reviver Himself. Higher Pursuits will position you to make ready the way of the Lord. This book is for the everyday revivalist who is ready for the one true longing of their soul to be satisfied by the Lover of their soul. This book is for the gal who wants to yield deeper in adoration, consecration, and desperation at the feet of her King Jesus!

Hailey Wall

TABLE OF CONTENTS

Introduction xi

Chapter 1: Higher Pursuit: Seek His Face 1

Chapter 2: Higher Pursuit: Fear of God (Awe & Wonder) 31

Chapter 3: Higher Pursuit: Biblical Worldview 65

Chapter 4: Higher Pursuit: Pursuit of Holiness 93

Chapter 5: Higher Pursuit: Holy Desperation 119

Chapter 6: Higher Pursuit: Filled with the Spirit 147

Final Thoughts 179

HI!
WELCOME TO THE JOURNEY OF HIGHER PURSUITS.

If you picked up a book with the word "revival" in it because that word stirs something in you, yet you just can't put your finger on it—*you are in the right place.*

If you read the book description that included intense phrases such as "fear of God" and "spiritual disciplines" and instantly swirled with excitement, then you are my people—*and you are in the right place.*

If you aren't quite sure what you would risk in the intimacy required to seek God's face much less risk in going after any Higher Pursuits and you picked up this book anyway because there's something in you that longs for more—*you are in the right place.*

If you are growing weary of lesser conversations on social media and in society at large that go after albeit important issues like comparison, jealousy, relationships, goal setting, purpose, etc., without getting to the root of each matter, and these lesser conversations without Higher Pursuits leave you frustrated—*you are in the right place.*

I know you've only just picked up this book and you don't know me from the next gal, but I'm going to ask you to do something weird. This is me inviting you into a vision the Lord gave me. I would love for you put yourself in this vision as the main character. I know it's weird, but it will be so good. I promise.

You find yourself on the edge of a cliff with running water below. The thing is, it's not you but rather a character of you. Remember playing Guess Who? or perhaps Candy Land as a kid? You are a square cardboard game piece on the edge of a cliff. And to make things a bit weirder, your face is on the game piece not as, say, a selfie from Instagram but as a cartoon character. And as you find your cartoon self at this cliff, something in you is off-kilter. In fact, your whole square is teetering on the tip of the square; at any moment you would tip over. Struggling, you are doing your very best to make yourself right, to get back on kilter, to get back as a right-up square—how you think you should be on the edge of this cliff.

And just as you grow tired of trying to get back to normal from this off-kilter state, you then fall into the running water below. This is not a treacherous fall though. It's glorious. Because, when you come out of the water, what was you in one-dimensional form now comes out of the water in your full self. Flat turns into 3D.

Now to make it even better, you come up out of the water (which I believe in the vision represented the presence of God) moving from uncertainty, stress, struggle, off-kilter into peace and confidence, full of God's glory, full of His love . . .

. . . *full of the Spirit of the living God.*

It's my desire to see the world, and especially Christian women, stop trying to get back to what once was before the world changed forever. That self-focused worship, self-focused Bible reading, obsession with goals and purpose, emotional un-health, stagnant faith—this must not be the state of the Church. It can't be! In the final chapter, I will get into what the Lord showed me next with this beautiful vision, but for now, I will encourage you that this journey of Higher Pursuits will position you to join in with what God is doing in this hour as you see revival and awakening in you and through you. To partner with God to bring light in this deep darkness is a Higher Pursuit worthy of your time and attention. To surrender to Christ on a deeper level than ever before because of your newfound awe and wonder through seeking His face is to come into faith that moves mountains and activates miracles. To be filled without measure of the power of the Holy Spirit is to live with boldness required to live out the gospel mandate.

If any of this gets you excited and ready to jump in the river and move from one dimensional faith straight into revival—***you are in the right place!***

Those who have read my previous books know that I require a bit of a pinky promise from you. I ask that you promise me you won't simply read this book. I ask that you interact with the scriptures I offer and actively dive into prayer and worship guided within the pages of this book. The Lord gave me a mandate years ago: to grab women by the hand and lead them into a vibrant life in the presence of Jesus where I simply facilitate a conversation. I then get to sit back and watch the glory ensue as you and the Lord embark on this journey of seeking Higher Pursuits together. How does that sound?

Each chapter of this book is set up to read day by day. Within each chapter you will find the following:

- A Higher Pursuit to focus on

- A Higher Pursuit to seek rather than the lesser conversations

- A name of God to sit with to enhance your worship

- A spiritual discipline to take you deeper in the act of growing your faith

- A challenge to make revival and awakening an everyday thing

In addition, each section of each chapter offers a mixture of study questions, journaling prompts, and prayer starters. This is where the rubber meets the road. Please don't skip them. You pinky promised!

Great. Go grab a journal. My favorite to use are cheap, good old-fashioned composition notebooks. Grab your journal and maybe even an app on your phone that provides a variety of Bible translations.

Come willing to forgo the lesser conversations, the lesser pursuits.

Position yourself humbly before Him with openness to be stretched, pruned, propelled in faith.

Let's get to it!

CHAPTER 1

HIGHER PURSUIT: SEEK HIS FACE

DAY 1: SHOW ME YOUR GLORY

My comfy prayer-room chair enveloped me as I sat with my Bible, journal, and a distracted mind. So much beauty surrounded me. My favorite art pieces on my inspiration wall served to remind me of that season when all I was called to do was to sit, wait in God's presence, mess around with paint by way of prayer, and let Him heal my ever-repentant heart. With a rich and recent history of meeting with the Lord to do deep soul work, I very much knew the delight of being filled with the Holy Spirit to search the things of God, to seek His face, to draw near. The problem: on this particular morning, my thoughts ping-ponged all over the room and I mindlessly grabbed my phone to scroll instead of press in.

I knew better. I knew the privilege of sitting in the presence of God, yet a social square grabbed my attention and affection in that moment. And soon, anger welled up. *Why in the world was I so easily distracted by lesser things?*

"Jesus, could You, would You just walk into this room right now?" That was my plea. I was certain that if I could quite literally see the face of

Jesus Himself, there was no way on God's green earth that anything else could distract my attention and affection.

I wish I could say that Jesus Himself walked into my art studio that morning. I mean, imagine what I could create with my watercolors after that encounter! My heart yearns for that kind of encounter. To see the face of Jesus even for a split second would wipe away any and all pursuits of the lesser, the temporary, and give me more vision for things above. One of my first-ever memory verses was Colossians 3:1-3, with the delineation between that which is temporary and that which is eternal. I'm a list person, so I'm all about any chance to make lists of earthly pursuits and heavenly pursuits.

> If then you have been raised with Christ, seek the things that are above, where Christ is, seated at the right hand of God. Set your minds on things that are above, not on things that are on earth. For you have died, and your life is hidden with Christ in God. When Christ who is your life appears, then you also will appear with him in glory. (Colossians 3:1-4)

Does this scripture provoke you to your own lists? If not, that's okay. By the end of this chapter, our hearts and minds will be oriented toward that higher pursuit of seeking the face of the Lord.

Our Higher Pursuit of *seeking the face of God* seems weird and unattainable. I mean, if we don't even know what the face of God looks like, how do we begin to seek Him out and seek His face? When we look at Old Testament context and original language, we find the meaning of the phrase "seek His face." These words lead us to topics of intimacy with God, of closeness, of drawing near in His presence. Throughout the psalms, David interchanges phrases that describe God's presence (intimacy and closeness to Him) with seeking His face.

> Hear, O Lord, when I cry aloud: be gracious to me and answer me! You have said, "Seek my face." My heart says to you, **"Your face, Lord, do I seek."** (Psalm 27:7-8, emphasis mine)

> Who shall ascend the hill of the Lord? And who shall stand in his holy place? He who has clean hands and a pure heart, who does not lift up his soul to what is false and does not swear deceitfully. He will receive blessing from the Lord and righteousness from the God of his salvation. Such is the generation of those who seek him, who **seek the face** of the God of Jacob. Selah. (Psalm 24:3-6, emphasis mine)

> You make known to me the path of life; **in your presence** there is fullness of joy; at your right hand are pleasures forevermore. (Psalm 16:11, emphasis mine)

In his book *Experiencing the Presence of God*, A. W. Tozer reminds us that "The Bible teaches that all of God's presence is everywhere. The Bible teaches that God's face—God's realized, manifest enjoyed presence—may be the precious treasure of all the people of God."

And while Jesus has yet to walk into my room and divinely turn my focus away from those pesky earthly distractions, the Holy Spirit comforts my disappointment. It is in the daily, even minute-by-minute choice to seek intimacy with Christ over any lesser thing that, in fact, stirs daily endurance to press in even when we just don't *feel* like it. James 4:8 reminds us that when we draw near to God, He will draw near to us. That everyday practice to ask God, "Show me Your glory!" as Moses declared in Exodus, positions us to see God Himself move in our lives on His best terms, not on our own conditions.

In Exodus 33 we read that God tells Moses He will show and display His glory and power, but His face was so holy that it would kill the human, Moses, should he look upon it. A man such as Moses who diligently worshiped and followed after God with abandon—this man couldn't even look upon the beauty of the Lord. This chapter in Exodus brings us to a point where the Israelites were wandering in the desert by the guiding of the Lord with a pillar of fire by night and a cloud by day. Day by day, God's very presence guided their journey. And just as humans do, they complained and took for granted all of the good, kind, merciful things God did for them as He miraculously moved the nation out of bondage in Egypt. But for Moses and his heartfelt, passionate plea, God would not have continued to cover Israel with His presence as they moved into His gift of the Promised Land.

> And the Lord said to Moses, "This very thing that you have spoken I will do, for you have found favor in my sight, and I know you by name." Moses said, "Please show me your glory." (Exodus 33:17-18)

When Moses discussed with God his holy desperation to move not one inch farther on the journey without God's presence, the Lord kindly agreed. And in that holy desperation, Moses begged to see for himself God's glory.

> And He said, "I will make all my goodness pass before you and will proclaim before you my name 'The Lord.' And I will be gracious to whom I will be gracious, and will show mercy on whom I will show mercy." (Exodus 33:19)

God equates His glory with the word "goodness." Let that wash over your soul right now. The weightiness of God's presence is translated in God's own words as His goodness that would pass over Moses. Moses declared that Israel would not go forward without God Himself. Moses' only desire was to seek God's face, to seek deep intimacy with nothing else but the Lord.

> But," he said, "you cannot see my face, for man shall not see me and live." And the Lord said, "Behold, there is a place by me where you shall stand on the rock, and while my glory passes by I will put you in a cleft of the rock, and I will cover you with my hand until I have passed by. Then I will take away my hand, and you shall see my back, but my face shall not be seen. (Exodus 33:21-23)

In His kindness and goodness (GLORY!), the Lord specifically directed Moses into where and how He would pass by and show him glory. At that time in biblical history, before Jesus changed everything, no one was able to see the pure beauty and righteousness of God's face. Thus, God directed Moses into the cleft of the rock and allowed him only to view His presence once He passed. It was on God's terms that Moses beheld glory.

How often do we ask to see God move in our life and then construct thick boundary lines around that desired movement? How often do we want to see God's movement in our lives but on our own terms and conditions? We might inadvertently proclaim, "It's only God if He moves within my preconceived notion of His glory and goodness," or "I've missed it, right? I must have missed it because it didn't look the way I thought it would!"

> *God's glory and goodness will not be contained in a box constructed by our limited human understanding.*

Instead, might we do well to seek His face, seek closeness with the Creator of our soul, by unclenching our grip and allowing Him to move how He best sees fit? Yes, I do believe so. Let's dive into the concept of seeking God's face together. Grab your pen and journal and work through these prompts.

Grab your Bible and read Exodus 33. How would you describe Moses and his desire for God's presence?

What was your definition of "seeking His face" before you started this book? (If you have never heard the term, that's okay!) How would you define the concept of God's glory and presence? This is just a baseline understanding. We are diving deeper in this very chapter.

HIGHER PURSUIT: SEEK HIS FACE

Have you constructed a box or drawn a line/boundary around what you think God's glory, power, love look like in your life?

What areas in your life do you know you need to declare, "Show me Your glory!"? How will you surrender as Moses did to the weightiness of God's goodness and glory?

DAY 2: GOLD VS. GLITTER

The Lord gave me this analogy when I was struggling to put words to these sometimes elusive concepts, such as God's presence, His glory, seeking His face: gold vs. glitter. This is a question I must daily ask the Lord to reveal: *Am I seeking Your face like I would value gold, or am I chasing after things of this world that distract and fade away like glitter?*

The original language of the word "glory" in the Old Testament is *kabod*, which refers to the weightiness of God's presence. We can associate weightiness with heaviness and value as well. You may have found yourself in a worship night where someone proclaimed that the presence of God was thick in the room. Have you ever wondered what that really means? Maybe this word picture will help.

I've never personally seen or held a block of gold, but society tells us that blocks of gold are extremely valuable. Based on movie heist scenes where thieves break into bank vaults and run out with big bags of stolen gold, I imagine that blocks of gold are heavy, smooth, and maybe feel cold to the touch. Weighty. Of high value. This is the word picture I use to grasp the value of God's presence, to seek His face with care, like I would hold a precious block of gold. It's also a question to ask daily: Do we, as people called to seek intimacy and closeness with God, value greatly *God's glory, presence, power*?

> **Do we hold the weight of God's presence like a block of gold, or do we seek out that which distracts and glitters?**

Have you ever received a prank greeting card where the sender encloses a ton of glitter or confetti that then explodes all over you? It's all well and fun until that glitter makes its way to every crevice of the room and is difficult to vacuum up. You still find glitter even months later. Or, what about a night when you wanted to have fun with your makeup and decided to grab your glitter eyeshadow. Guaranteed, by the middle of dinner that glitter is all up in your eyes and messing with your contacts. Glitter is fun but quickly distracting.

"Distraction"—that's an important word in our conversation about idols (stay tuned for the next Higher Pursuit) and especially about what we view as valuable. In any given moment, glittery, temporary things that we allow to take our focus/attention/affection—that divert our eyes and distract—rob us of deep immersion in God's presence and thus rob us of deeper intimacy with the only One who is called Everlasting. Glittery lesser pursuits keep us in the temporal. Seeking His face and valuing God's glory keep us with eyes on the everlasting. To be honest, that's tricky. If we don't have a grasp on the depth of goodness and satisfaction in what is eternal, those glittery pursuits cause us to believe this is the best it's going to get right here and now. Let's take note from David who wrote rich scripture instructing and exhorting us to hold in value God's presence and glory through the act of seeking His face.

Since the psalms are full of verses and declarations to seek the face of God, I think it's fitting that we talk about King David and his intimacy with God. Given that he had access to the best scholars, priests, and Levites (those who served in the temple to minister directly to the Lord), it is safe to say that David had an abundance of knowledge *about* God. Just as many of us who live in countries with easy access to Bibles and, at the least, Youtube sermons, it would be hard to find many people who do not know about Him. But David had more than simple head knowledge; David had experiential soul and spirit history with his Creator, the One who wove him intricately in his mother's womb (see Psalm 139). I've often wondered what exactly was the catalyst for David's deep, true, steadfast relationship with Yahweh—Emmanuel, God with us. Might it be that David simply heard God's voice in the quiet solitude of the field while tending sheep? One who is called "a man after God's heart" in Scripture doesn't come by that lightly. Hearing God's voice—developing a tenderness for connection and communion with our Creator—and thus a desperation to seek His face isn't limited to the king of Israel. Taking notes from David's psalms and recorded history of devotion might provoke us to value God's presence. I believe David sought intimacy with God as more than just a feeling or a Holy Spirit high of emotions. Out of necessity, it was a choice to keep ever so close with Him. Might he have lived so close that he could see what was reflected in the eye of God Almighty? I think so.

Along with scriptures such as Psalm 24, where David heralds the abundant blessing bestowed upon those with clean hands and a pure heart, those who seek the face of the one and only God, Psalm 16 gives us a life outline to lead us into true soul and spirit knowledge of the value of God's presence and glory. Let's take notes from this instructive psalm of David, Psalm 16:1-11:

> Preserve me, O God, for in you I take refuge.
> I say to the Lord, "You are my Lord;
>   I have no good apart from you."

Decide to dip into only one well of goodness as you put a stake in the ground to forsake the glittery idols and worship only Jesus. The giver of good and perfect gifts from above sets us apart to overflow His goodness and be a blessing to the world.

> As for the saints in the land, they are the excellent ones,

> in whom is all my delight.
> The sorrows of those who run after another god shall multiply;
>> their drink offerings of blood I will not pour out
>> or take their names on my lips.
> The Lord is my chosen portion and my cup;
>> you hold my lot.

Declare to your own soul to live as a committed daughter following only the One who took our sin and sorrows to the cross. No other god rose from the grave to defeat sin and death. Only Jesus! This declaration to the depths of your soul makes its way there through the Holy Spirit highlighting the precious treasure of a chosen portion: God's presence, His glory, His goodness.

But do you see the choice available at any given moment? A higher pursuit to seek the face of God over the lesser things that lack depth and value.

> The lines have fallen for me in pleasant places;
>> indeed, I have a beautiful inheritance.

In His goodness, the Lord draws boundary lines. The Word of God is not a book of no's or not-yets but a divine invitation to God's best design for His creation. Through the guidance of the Holy Spirit, a life pursuing God's best positions us in abundance—not void of suffering, but full of His never depleting power, love, mercy, forgiveness, provision, comfort.

> I bless the Lord who gives me counsel;
>> in the night also my heart instructs me.

> I have set the Lord always before me;
>> because he is at my right hand, I shall not be shaken.

Yes, again David makes the active choice to honor and seek God alone. With the use of the original language for "bless," *barak*, David blesses the Lord with a word defined to honor, praise, adore, and kneel. Time and again, David, a man of great power yet often in harm's way, blesses and kneels before God. For counsel, instruction, love, comfort, David determines to set the Lord before him to follow only God. Imagine that, a king who could require Israel to follow him and kneel before his authority lives himself under devotion and submission to God, Jehovah—the Existing One.

> Therefore my heart is glad, and my whole being rejoices;
>> my flesh also dwells secure.
>
> For you will not abandon my soul to Sheol,
>> or let your holy one see corruption.
>
> You make known to me the path of life;
>> in your presence there is fullness of joy;
>> at your right hand are pleasures forevermore. (Psalm 16:1-11)

The word "choice" again is interesting. By choosing, declaring, deciding, David sets himself up for the highest counsel and security in God's presence. But he is not referring to some far-off, ethereal concept of God's presence. In fact, the word used for life in this passage isn't one meaning, say, eternal life, far off life after death. No, David literally states that God's good hand leads him to actual, tangible life decisions here and now. The path forward was not always clear for David, as he was often pursued by enemies or fighting off adversaries. Through uncertainty and often physical and emotional pain, David sought God for step-by-step provision and direction. And even yet again, he declares through original Hebrew words that the very presence (God's face!) secured David overflowing, full joy.

I'm challenged and encouraged after studying this psalm to forsake glittery distractions that set me up to for a life that is fake and not authentic. Through easy clicks of selfies, added filters, complimentary edits and crops, heart counts, the illusion that we are seen and known traps us into chasing after that which leaves us empty: the lesser things. However, higher pursuit of seeking God's face is never a journey in vain. Like David's soul choices and declarations, the journey is full of decisions to make daily. We will get into the work Jesus did on the cross and His ultimate price paid in the following section, but for today, do you see the vulnerability displayed by David time and again in Scripture? That level of trust to draw near comes from time put in—choices every minute to value God's presence and behold Him with care and attention.

This is not just a chore for a good Bible girl to search the things of God—to seek His face—and check the box of daily devotion. But instead, there's a divine invitation to behold God Himself and search the depths of His nature and character and, of course, to let Him speak His everlasting love for us. I think we hear the heroes of the faith talk about their love for the Lord and extraordinary experiences with the Holy Spirit. Do you hear their stories and think it's all and well for them but you could never know God with such intimacy? Lean in; this is important to grasp: the faith of an A. W. Tozer, a Lou Engle, or a Corrie ten Boom is not unattainable. I believe they would tell you that their secret to searching and seeking God's face is not a secret at all. It's a commitment to devotion.

> *To value is to hold precious. To hold precious is to recognize the cost. To recognize the cost is to view as worthy.*

To view as worthy is to treasure. To treasure is to hide in your heart and be found hidden in Christ alone.

Choose to hold on to the block of gold even if that means turning away from that which glitters and distracts.

And really, it's a simple yet not simple desire to explore when you actively seek the face of God—just like you would ask questions and follow-up questions and go deep with even more dialogue to get to know a treasured new friend. This is the pursuit of God. Let the Spirit of the living God lead you in the journey through His Word to ask questions:

- Lord, who do You say You are?

- Lord, show me the nuances of Your beauty and love.

- Tell me what is on Your mind today.

- Tell me what is on Your heart today.

- Lord, teach me to walk close in Your presence.

I believe the Lord who smiles when He says your name will be quick to answer these questions and declarations.

And on the flip side, just as you would seek, ask, probe deeper, a valuable relationship can't be one-sided. How do we become a friend of God and hold His presence like gold, not glitter? It requires vulnerability on our end, too:

Holy Spirit, here I am with my heart splayed before You. I will let You in. Fill me. Search me. Cleanse me. Teach me. Love me, Lord. I let You in.

HIGHER PURSUIT: SEEK HIS FACE

Grab your pen, journal, and Bible to work through these prompts. Let the Holy Spirit take you deeper.

Let's get real and raw. What is the glitter in your life right now? Let the Holy Spirit kindly convict you. It's okay; in the uncovering you will make room for the gold—more of God's glory and goodness instead of that which will for sure disappoint and leave you dissatisfied.

What comes to mind as you unpack the analogy of God's weightiness (glory and presence) to be valued like a precious block of gold?

Read Psalm 16 straight through and then re-read my breakdown and commentary above. How can you bless God? What can you declare? How have those boundary lines fallen in pleasant places?

Write out a prayer using verses Psalm 16 as your guide.

DAY 3: CHARACTER OF GOD/NAME OF GOD: JESUS AS HIGH PRIEST

But for Jesus . . . our High Priest.

It's a concept hard to grasp as a modern, Western, and New Covenant believer. Even still, let's look at that a little more closely. Every year during Holy Week you might read on Good Friday the scripture describing Jesus' horrific death on the cross of Calvary. As He was nailed to the cross and as He took His last breath, Jesus proclaimed, "It is finished." And at that moment, things shifted for you and me as daughters of God. We read that the veil was torn. What does this mean?

To answer that question, let's start from the beginning, shall we? Starting at the genesis of time helps us to remember, recognize, live in the reality of what once was and what Christ sacrificed to bring us back into full fellowship with God Himself.

Adam and Eve walked in the cool of the day, in the cool of the garden with Yahweh, LORD, Jehovah, Elohim—Creator. Does this stir a longing for intimacy with God? If it doesn't quite do just that, let these words paint a picture of what once was and what is reality should we decide to seek the face of God.

Adam and Eve were formed with care and passion by the Creator of the universe. As the only two created ones bearing the image of God, they lived in full fellowship with the lover of their souls. Without the distractions of social squares to numb out or fantastical binge-worthy shows to divert their imagination and attention, Adam and Even lived fully present in the beauty of the garden of Eden. They lived fully present in relationship with Elohim—God the creator. If there ever was a definition of "intentional living," as we like to say, Adam and Eve knew no other than the heavenly realities of being a friend of God—a son and daughter with full access to the One who flung the stars in the sky and laid depth to the sea all by the sound of His voice.

Peace. Assurance of His voice. In the shade of the tree that God created for exactly that purpose—rest in His presence to seek His face and know His glory and goodness.

When our soul's desire is for some sort of rest and reprieve from the hard, edgy world, we may not even know the prescription for that shalom-peace is closeness to God—so close as to see our reflection in His eye.

We know that sin entered the picture when Adam and Eve decided there must be more, that maybe God was holding out on them by holding back the fruit of the forbidden tree. With this doubt of God's goodness, a foothold for Satan was formed to plant lies and doubt.

And as they partook in the fruit—an act of disobedience and distrust—those with soul-satisfying connection to their Creator were now separate from Him. God—the One whose face and intimacy they knew as reality—in His righteousness and holiness could no longer be in fellowship because of their sin. Even still, God's love moved Him to clothe the once free and naked Adam and Eve so they would not live in their shame and guilt.

Through time and covenant and promises made to God's chosen people, sacrifices of the blood of innocent animals were required to make one right before God. A law was prescribed to display God's utmost holiness and man's human inability to meet the law requirements. Altars, temporary tabernacles for worship, then magnificent temples were erected and built. In His kindness and righteousness, holiness, purity, magnificence, God chose to dwell among His people.

This brings us to Jesus, our Great High Priest, on the cross. It is finished. The veil was torn.

In the ancient temple of Jesus' day, the Most Holy was the place where God's presence dwelt—God Himself in His weighty, powerful glory was separate from even the rest of the temple where the Jews worshiped. Only one priest, once a year, ritually cleansed to be made worthy, could approach what we now know as the throne of grace (see Hebrews 4:16). This veil mentioned in the Good Friday accounts within the Gospels wasn't some decorative curtain like we hang in our homes. No, it was a thick, tall wall to separate God's presence from His creation.

When Jesus took His last breath on the cross and cried, "It is finished," the veil in the temple that separated humanity from God's holy presence was torn not by human hands but through the blood shed by Jesus our Messiah, who brings us back to our loving Father. Our sins were covered by His love. Because of Jesus, no longer would we be separated from God. A holy Father God sent His precious Son to enter into our humanity and our sin, and His death brought us back to what once was: fellowship, closeness, *face-to-face* proximity to our Creator. Just as Adam and Eve walked in the cool of the day with God, we too walk in this shalom-peace closeness with Him when we surrender to Jesus as Savior.

The cool of the day with God is ours because of Jesus.

The pursuit of seeking the face of God Himself is made ours because of Jesus.

The access to the weighty, precious glory of God Himself is because of Jesus.

Because of Jesus, we can draw near to the throne of grace to find mercy, forgiveness, undeserved favor (grace), help, comfort, provision, direction to not go at this life alone—to seek the very face of God Himself.

> For it was indeed fitting that we should have such a high priest, holy, innocent, unstained, separated from sinners, and exalted above the heavens. He has no need, like those high priests, to offer sacrifices daily, first for his own sins and then for those of the people, since he did this once for all when he offered up himself. For the law appoints men in their weakness as high priests, but the word of the oath, which came later than the law, appoints a Son who has been made perfect forever. (Hebrews 7:26-28)

Jesus our High Priest changes everything.

Grab your pen, journal, and Bible.

Today's prompt is simple. Grab a couple of different translations (via Google or your Bible app—or even a couple of different Bibles that you might have on your shelf). Take some time to prayerfully write the Word. Without allowing yourself to zone out, let the Holy Spirit stir the words of life in your spirit as you write out Hebrews 7:26-28 in a couple of different Bible translations.

DAY 4: SPIRITUAL DISCIPLINE: PRAYER—NOT A DUTY BUT A DELIGHT

I can't string together words to convince you of the value of God's presence in your life—the value of that intimacy in knowing your loving Father face to face. Any words I pose to you will fall short in teaching or grounding you in what only meeting with Him will unveil.

This is where prayer comes into play.

Hebrews 11:6 tells us that those who seek God Himself, who He is, what His character and nature are, those people will be rewarded—with His presence. We look at Hebrews 11 as the faith chapter, and the Bible heroes mentioned had one thing in common: By faith, these men and women believed God to be the one and only God. This shaped their faith. It framed their vision for life. They sought after who God is and believed Him to be the one and only. No other god would capture their heart, affection, and worship.

On this side of heaven, there is no way to really know the depths of the devotional prayer life of heroes like Moses, Abraham, Sarah, Esther, David, or Deborah. I can't imagine those so empowered by God were not in regular conversation—prayer—with Him.

I also think of Anna and Simeon, who devoted their lives to waiting for their Messiah so much so that Anna never left the temple and her life was found centered around prayer and worship. What a reward for faithful prayer to then be blessed as she laid eyes on Jesus as a baby—the One her soul longed for.

Prayer brings us face to face with the One our soul longs for.

Jesus valued communion and time alone with His Father as He awoke early in the morning to rest and refresh in God's presence. He even taught us to pray too.

Our Father, Hallowed be Your name

Lifting up with reverence, awe, and wonder the name of God positions us rightly as we come into prayer.

Your Kingdom come, Your will be done on earth as it is in heaven.

His will, His agenda, His heavenly realities are what the whole earth groans for.

Give us this day our daily bread,

Day by day, with dependence on the only One who satisfies our needs and desires. Might we also feed on His Word that is our bread of life?

And forgive us our trespasses as we forgive those who trespass against us.

The confession of sin and the act of repentance clear away any barriers that set us apart from full fellowship with the Father.

Lead us not into temptation, but deliver us from evil. (Matthew 6:9-13)

The recognition of temptation, the recognition of our bent to turn away from God's best, this choice to lean into the freedom from sin found in the power of the Holy Spirit draws us closer as we deny our self-focused desires. I wonder what victory chants are played in heaven each time God's children take up their cross, deny their sin, and follow Jesus' better way of surrender, love, power, mercy!

As we work through the pages of this book together, my hope is that your desire to seek God's face will burn like a refining fire. Let prayer be the ember that stokes the flame. There are days when we just don't feel like coming before the Lord. There are days when our hearts are so tender that we might not trust God's goodness to hold us with kindness. There are also days when temptation swirls and shame keeps us from running back to confess and repent. This is the turning away from temptation and sin and the turning toward God's best. And there are days when we don't feel His presence and complacency creeps in. These are all real scenarios and this is where prayer bridges the gap that seems so wide between you and the Father. As you simply show up, you will find that gap isn't as wide as you think and you haven't fallen too far so as to miss your window to draw near and seek the face of God for restoration.

There are multitudes of books about prayer at our fingertips these days. The best I can offer you in our time together in this book is the invitation to *just show up*. You will find that as you pursue higher things of God, your prayer language and holy heart habit will grow and flourish. He rewards those who diligently seek Him!

Want to go ahead and jump in? It doesn't have to be complicated. I will offer a couple of tools for you. Grab a journal, a pen, and your Bible. Simple as that. Below you will find prayer starters, and I challenge you to put pen to paper. It is the holistic act of moving our hands with pen and paper to actively engage the Lord that keeps our mind from wandering. By moving pen on paper to confess, to hear His voice, to write out scripture, our heart, soul, mind, strength are engaged within the pages of a love letter written back and forth from God to His daughter adored.

You might find your mind wanders. That's okay. Just write out what is wandering and ask the Holy Spirit to speak into your daily stress and distractions. If you get stuck and don't know what to write out, start by transcribing scripture onto the pages of your journal. His Word brings fire when complacency creeps in. The Word made flesh—Jesus—will meet you there in your act of holding that life force with reverence as you write the Word.

We will build on the discipline of prayer throughout this book as we add in worship, confession, repentance, fasting, scripture memorization. But for this moment, let's simply approach the throne of grace and seek the face of God in prayer. Let these prayer points serve as just a starting point. Give yourself permission to allow the Holy Spirit to move as you scribble your prayers on paper. Let it be messy and raw. Let your heart tenderize and then burn for closeness to God Himself. Draw near. Walk in the cool of the day with Him. Seek His face.

Grab your journal, pen, and Bible.

Prayer points to get you started as the Spirit leads you:

Lord, show me more of who You are…

I might know You in my head as loving, kind, good, powerful. Lord, from the depths of my soul, let Your Spirit reveal the depths of who You are…

Forgive me…

HIGHER PURSUITS

I repent I turn to You instead...

Thank You for the cross, Jesus!

Help me to see where I value lesser things that glitter and distract. ...I confess...

Give me eyes to see behold Your glory...

Give me a heart for You alone...

DAY 5: EVERYDAY REVIVAL: TIME IS OF THE ESSENCE

As I stated in the introduction, revival isn't some lofty, unattainable ideal. It's an encounter with the living God as you are moved by the Holy Spirit in unabashed worship and surrender. We will build up to what revival looks like on a national and global scale as we move through these Higher Pursuits, and in chapter 7 you will be equipped on how to pray and live revival ready.

Time is of the essence.

This phrase is often used to light a fire and motivate people toward a greater goal or deadline. This phrase also creates a sense of urgency. As one who loves to power through and check the boxes of accomplishments and to-do lists, urgent statements such as "time is of the essence" speak to my soul. Though this motivating phrase is used to propel us forward due to limited, precious, valuable time, I also see it as a prophetic statement to encourage us as women on a higher pursuit. We talked about the necessity to weigh and evaluate how we personally value and hold precious God's glory and presence. Intimacy with God Himself must not be only attained in our designated quiet time or set-aside prayer closet. How we spend our time, our emotional capital, our social capital, our financial capital, our brain space indicates whether we are flitting around with glitter or holding tenderly our relationship with Christ and allowing the Spirit to guide us, counsel us, fill us with God's presence.

Everyday revival is sparked by surrendering our time and attention to the One who bests orders our day out of His perfect love and wisdom. But before a realignment of our priorities comes, there must be a holy alignment and understanding of Who it is we devote our time, attention, and affection to. As much as I have tried over the years to paint a picture of God's presence with my words, as much as I've thrown paint on a canvas to somehow capture His glory with color, the Holy Spirit best speaks through the Word of God to give me a visual that then propels me toward holding my time in the balance to glorify God and offer my life as a living sacrifice, as in Romans 12.

Will you let the words of this scripture open the door of your imagination? Everyday revival and restoration are coupled with a readiness to seek His face, led by the Holy Spirit and guided by His Word penned long ago by one who is self-proclaimed as the beloved disciple—John. That bold title in and of itself provokes me toward affections and depth of relationship with Jesus to be called His beloved! We are His beloved. Behold Who it is you are loved by:

> At once I was in the Spirit, and behold, a throne stood in heaven, with one seated on the throne. And he who sat there had the appearance of jasper and carnelian, and around the throne was a rainbow that had the appearance of an emerald. Around the throne were twenty-four thrones, and seated on the thrones were twenty-four elders, clothed in white garments, with golden crowns on their heads. From the throne came flashes of lightning, and rumblings and peals of thunder, and before the throne were burning seven torches of fire, which are the seven spirits of God, and before the throne, there was as it were a sea of glass, like crystal. (Revelation 4:2-6)

Go ahead, grab your pen. I invite you to write in this book. Ask the Holy Spirit to stir your imagination to translate these words into your pictures in your own mind. Underline what stirs you most. Then grab your journal and Bible and start writing out the verses/phrases with your own descriptions of God's glory and majesty. You will feel inadequate at first. It's okay. The act of interacting with the Spirit and the Word keeps you engaged, mind, soul, heart, and strength. Let's keep reading:

> And around the throne, on each side of the throne, are four living creatures, full of eyes in front and behind: the first living creature like a lion, the second living creature like an ox, the third living creature with the face of a man, and the fourth living creature like an eagle in flight. And the four living creatures, each of them with six wings, are full of eyes all around and within, and day and night they never cease to say, "Holy, holy, holy, is the Lord God Almighty, who was and is and is to come!" And whenever the living creatures give glory and honor and thanks to him who is seated on the throne, who lives forever and ever, the twenty-four elders fall down before him who is seated on the throne and worship him who lives forever and ever. They cast their crowns before the throne, saying, "Worthy are you, our Lord and God, to receive glory and honor and power, for you created all things, and by your will they existed and were created." (Revelation 4:6-11)

Take note of the depth of praise and devotion. These heavenly throne room creatures and saints spent day after day, hour after hour—investing their time—in praise of God sitting on this throne covered in unfathomable glory and beauty. Imagine the color. Imagine the sounds of instruments. Might there be color we have yet to see with earthly eyes? Might there be notes we've yet to sing with earthly limited voices?

Time in His presence became the essence of their existence.

An encounter with this God is what stokes the flame of everyday, along-the-way revival. You and I aren't called to live a monastic life sequestered in a beautiful monastery in the hills of a foreign land to live in solitude and worship. Somedays I do dream of the shalom-peace available in those spaces. But on this side of heaven, what would it look like to order our days, our agendas, our tasks, and goals to live as women glorifying God with our gifts and talents while also continually proclaiming, "Holy, holy, holy is the Lord God Almighty, who was and is and is to come!"

Our life doesn't have to be *either* monastic *or* in the world. It isn't either/or type of living: monk sequestered or successful woman of the world. It's actually a both/and. Let me explain why. By positioning ourselves to daily, minute by minute seek the face of God in the mundane tasks of our to-do list as well as the exciting accomplishments of our goals, we create space for His beauty, divine inspiration, and love to cover and enrich our day. In holding God's presence and desire to live ever so close to Him (handling the gold versus the glitter), we become vessels of His glory to shine out and bless the world around us.

Just as we read in Isaiah 6:1 that the train of God's robe fills the temple and the weighty presence of the Lord covers the space, because of Jesus—our High Priest—we now live as a temple of the living God to which "the whole earth is filled with His glory" (Isaiah 6:2). To be this vessel that expands her heart, soul, mind, and strength for the glory and goodness to be housed, an investment of our time and affection must be made. Go ahead and take these prompts to the Lord and allow the Holy Spirit to move your affections specifically in regard to how you spend your days, how you linger in your thoughts, how you align your priorities. We will continue to build on this concept of everyday revival in our journey of Higher Pursuits. But for now, let's get down and dirty and evaluate our time and attention.

HIGHER PURSUIT: SEEK HIS FACE

Grab your pen, journal, and Bible.

Take some time to map out how you spend a normal day. This will take diligence, but it is worth it. Place your time in category buckets, such as work, family, fun, worship/devotion/prayer/the Word, rest, planning, chores, exercise, indulgences.

Journal through what the Spirit stirred in you while reading Revelation 4. Write out your own words of adoration and praise to the Lord. This word picture of God offers holy motivation to offer our time/affection/attention to the Lord in our every day.

Does this Higher Pursuit of seeking the face of God—seeking closeness in His glory and presence—lead you to spend more of your time, attention, affection in His presence? How do you see yourself going about every day (the mundane and even the exciting and fun) while valuing God's glory like gold? When are you most susceptible to seeking the glittery things of your day?

Prayer prompts:

Holy Spirit, will You move my heart, soul, and spirit to a deeper understanding and revelation of Your glory? Show me Your glory…

HIGHER PURSUITS

Lord, show me what the fruit of a life seeking Your face looks like when I put my time and affection toward seeking Your face in my every day...

Thank You for...

CHAPTER 2

HIGHER PURSUIT: FEAR OF GOD (AWE & WONDER)

DAY 1: THE PURSUIT OF BOTH/AND

She sat with a death grip on her idol. Sometimes (all the time) emotions such as fear soaked in adrenaline mixed in with a fight-or-flight mechanism are easier to hang on to than the thought of even remotely trusting God.

It's Christmas time and she sees cutesie decorative signs drenched with glitter. The signs say "Awe & Wonder" with snowflakes and maybe a cross adorning the wood. With a weary heart, she questions everything about the season. Awe and wonder of what exactly? Who? God? "Nah," she says, "isn't God someone to be feared or to turn away from in shame?" To her, "awe and wonder"-sounds obscure. What is *awe-some* about a person I can't even see? What is *wonder-full* about this God I've only known to lay down the law of shoulds and should-nots?

She finds herself in the pews yet another Sunday morning. Frustrated. There must be more than this. All these songs thinly veiled with praise and thanksgiving are really worship of self. She is growing tired of singing about what God does "for me." Something in her tweaks with yet another self-focused morning of worship and prayer. Because, don't we all come to the end of ourselves quickly? She knows that "self-help" theology and worship have failed her, but what now?

If I were sitting on my couch with any of these gals, I would first offer up a hot beverage and my beloved, infamous dog, Lucy, for cuddles while we talk. Why the warm and fuzzy first? Because we would get down to the nitty-gritty real quick: fear of God. And as you read the pages of this book, nothing I could ever say would compel you to fear God with reverence, with awe and wonder. I could yell it from the rooftops, but it might just echo hollow as if I were yelling into a vast, empty canyon. My words are void if not coupled with God's Word and driven by the Holy Spirit. And most importantly, if not for the cross of Christ, we would have only head knowledge of God Himself. Because of His blood shed for the sickness of our sins, to make us right and holy before the Holy One, we can move from knowledge with intellect and intertwine spirit and soul wisdom as Paul prayed in Ephesians 1:17-21.

> ... that the God of our Lord Jesus Christ, the Father of glory, may give you the **Spirit of wisdom** and of **revelation in the knowledge of him**, having the **eyes of your hearts enlightened**, that you may **know** what is the **hope to which he has called you**, what are the riches of his glorious **inheritance in the saints**, and what is the **immeasurable greatness** of his power toward us who

believe, according to the working of his great might that he worked **in Christ when he raised him from the dead and seated him at his right hand in the heavenly places**, far above all rule and authority and power and dominion, and above every name that is named, not only in this age but also in the one to come. (Ephesians 1:17-21, emphasis mine)

The pursuit of self only takes us so far. Especially in a world where we've seen the Lord shake out, shake in, and shake through over the past several years. The inferior pursuit of knowledge of self leaves you hanging empty, but the Spirit of wisdom and revelation in the knowledge of God *Himself* brings us into right understanding of where true glory and goodness is found—and it's not found in the lesser pursuits of self that have creeped their way into even the church. But rather, our higher pursuits bring us to . . .

Awe and wonder spark delight, exploration, curiosity, a search for more because the soul recognizes its shallowness without the depth of God Himself. Scripture describes even Jesus and His awe and wonder of the Father: "And his delight shall be in the fear of the Lord" (Isaiah 11:3).

Reverence offers a positioning of heart, soul, mind, and strength to go low and bow only before the one true God and not any other delights that set themselves above God, who is worthy of awe and wonder.

Fear of God Himself is a lifestyle of choices. It's a lifestyle not of earthly fear that brings death but of a choice in heavenly, divine fear when you seek the human-blinding glory of the Creator of the universe with eyes opened by the blood of Christ on the cross of Calvary. It's a lifestyle to choose heaven or hell—intertwined with the love of the Father eternally or the horrific separation from God's presence that sustains, delights, fulfills, and quenches our soul. It's an earthly choice to live in awe and wonder while bowing low in utmost respect and honor to God alone and no other idol.

But to move into Paul's words from Ephesians 1 and to operate in the Spirit of wisdom and revelation brings us into a lifestyle enthralled with the higher pursuit of the fear of God. A foundational, right understanding guided by the Holy Spirit through the truth of the Word—this is what is in order for the hour we live in. As we learned to seek intimacy with God and to seek His face in chapter 1, naturally a fear of God comes into play. All higher pursuits after that must come from the desire of intimacy with the Father and a right understanding of His awe and wonder. A lifestyle of seeking His face daily. A lifestyle of fear and reverence. These are our first and most highest pursuits.

I want to let you in on something I'm seeing these days. It's a sneaky phenomenon happening in the church especially within the past decade. In a world where not only politics is divided into left, right, blue, red, conservative vs. liberal, a fear of God is lost in this world of extremes we live in. And what I'm about to say implicates both conservative and liberal/progressive church mindsets. Through the decades, many have only spoken and waved fingers, stirring fire and brimstone about the righteous, judging, powerful God of the Bible. In all fairness, we see that holiness and righteousness spelled out in the Old Testament. But with legalistic mindsets, that fire and judgment in many circles is the only facet of God preached. Hang with me here, okay?

On the flip side, and just as egregious, we see a swing toward preaching and teaching that only cover the love and mercy of God. We hear progressives negate the holiness and due reverence of God to only focus on the mercy Christ chose by dying on the cross. With redefinitions of sin and the negating of the Old Testament narrative, we find a savior—the Lamb of God—without the talk of God's holiness, righteousness, and purity. In these teachings, the good news of the cross and resurrection is centered on Christ's *obedience* to death while leaving out God's righteousness and wrath toward sin.

The problem is, neither of these extremes covers the vastness and grandeur of the depths of God's character and nature. Neither takes into account that Jesus is *both* the Lamb that was slain *and* the Lion of Judah coming again in vengeance over death, sin, evil—Satan. And in our errant, Western mindset of extremes, we have drawn a tragic box around our understanding of God. We have become an *either/or* church of believers, not a *both/and*.

Hear me say, there are very clear lines to draw in the sand regarding Scripture and there are absolute truths that are non-negotiable regarding what the Word of God says about His nature and character. We will cover them in the higher pursuit of biblical worldview. But, might our human-limited understanding of God have trapped us into forgetting that . . .

God is *both* righteous, holy, full of wrath *and* merciful, kind, forgiving, full of love.

Both sides of the coin are valid. The Western mindset is to hang tight to and draw lines around the concept that either God is righteous, holy, full of wrath *or* He is simply/only merciful, kind, abundant in love. And by looking at the character of God that way, we limit our own understanding of His fullness. He is *both*! Let's allow Scripture to break open the box of our understanding as we pair both/and verses together. As you read, go ahead and grab your pen and circle any word such as "holiness," "righteousness," "love," "mercy," etc. Let's actively dive into the Word to get straight to the source that tells us who God is.

> Who is like you, O Lord, among the gods? Who is like you, majestic in holiness, awesome in glorious deeds, doing wonders? (Exodus 15:11)

> For God so loved the world, that he gave his only Son, that whoever believes in him should not perish but have eternal life. (John 3:16)

> Worship the Lord in the splendor of holiness; tremble before him, all the earth! (Psalm 96:9)

> He has delivered us from the domain of darkness and transferred us to the kingdom of his beloved Son, in whom we have redemption, the forgiveness of sins. (Colossians 1:13-14)

> Who will not fear, O Lord, and glorify your name? For you alone are holy. All nations will come and worship you, for your righteous acts have been revealed. (Revelation 15:4)

> For the wages of sin is death, but the free gift of God is eternal life in Christ Jesus our Lord. (Romans 6:23)

I started our Higher Pursuits journey with *seeking His face* by way of creating intimacy and closeness in order that we might then cultivate a fear of God. To see Him rightly is to get so close that the awe and wonder of who God is brings us to our knees to worship God alone. The Word of God offers us descriptions, stories, biblical/world history, and teaching in order to then guide us to seek *the knowledge of the glory of God in the face of Christ Jesus (because of the cross!) and by the power of the Holy Spirit.*

This is our highest pursuit. This is what aligns us to lead a life pursuing God's best design for us as His children. All else will lead us to trade and sell out abundance for flat, false gods that set themselves up higher than our one and only—our one true love.

Read these last two scriptures that mirror each other from the Old Testament and the New Testament, then grab your journal to work it through some more.

God's righteousness:

> For the earth will be filled with the knowledge of the glory of the Lord as the waters cover the sea. (Habakkuk 2:14)

God's love, mercy, forgiveness:

> The God who spoke light into existence, saying, "Let light shine from the darkness," is the very One who sets our hearts ablaze to shed light on the knowledge of God's glory revealed in the face of Jesus, the Anointed One. (2 Corinthians 4:6, The Voice Translation)

Grab your journal, pen, and Bible.

For context, the verse from Habakkuk 2:14 surrounds God's glory shining in His perfect judgment

over sin and death—over those who operated in evil. Then, on the other side of the cross, we find 2 Corinthians 2:14, which offers the knowledge of God's glory, power, righteousness, and merciful love in the face of the Savior, Christ Jesus.

We covered the fact that we can seek God's face and come into awe and wonder because of Jesus' finished work on the cross and in His resurrection. Describe your thoughts on the fear of God and the weight of His glory in the face of Jesus, as in 2 Corinthians 4:6.

In the original language, the word "knowledge" (see Habakkuk 2:14) describes "experiencing" God's glory. How do you see the higher pursuit of fear of the Lord enriched by experiencing the weight of God's glory?

Did any boxes that you drew around God's character and nature break open by reading the both/and scriptures above? What side of the coin did you mostly find yourself in before? What stretched your mindset and worship by looking at both the righteousness of God and His love/mercy?

DAY 2: REAL TALK ABOUT IDOLS

Same comfy chair, same blanket, same prayer space except this is six years ago and, unbeknownst to me, my soul was about to be laid bare. I heard the Lord whisper to my heart...

Put it away.

In a matter of seconds my heart, soul, and mind were relieved of the idol of accomplishment. I willingly set it down. I set it aside because the "good Jesus girl" in me knows that idols make a jealous God angry. And to be honest, I willingly set this idol to the side because my arms were too tired to lift it up any longer. I was weary. I was tired of building my own kingdom and propping up myself for success. I was worn out from the rejection that inevitably comes when going after those glittery pursuit. So I willingly laid down the idol.

But soon, the Holy Spirit handed me a holy hammer to crash that thing to pieces. Seems violent? Yes. At times, the pain from unclenching that which I held so dear was unnerving.

I was geared up to start another project for work. It was time to get cracking in order to stay relevant. The clock was ticking. I scraped and scratched for any topic I could put words to in order to then hopefully publish. Yeah, that idol of accomplishment and relevance is a slippery little fella when it convinces you that doing "good works" is, well, good, no matter the timing or the anointing from God—or lack thereof.

Though I would never want anyone else to find their hands calloused from gripping tightly to this same idol (or any other one for that matter), I'm thinking you might very well understand that tension of holding tightly to what strokes your ego and the deep knowledge that very same act of stroking the ego depletes your soul. Ego vs. soul. Relevance vs. hiding. Striving vs. abiding. Achievement vs. rest. Shallowness vs. the depths of God's glory found in seeking His face rather than that which temporarily holds you up to an earthly standard that is ever-changing.

We are going to progress through some scriptures and concepts to set us up in our Higher Pursuit of fear of the Lord and to tear down the lesser pursuits of idols—those things we set up against the knowledge and the glory of God alone.

> Knowledge of God's glory——> fear of God
> Fear of God——> awe and wonder
> Awe and wonder——> to see Him rightly
> To see Him rightly——> reveals our own sin and brokenness
> The blood of Jesus on the cross covered our sin——> back to fullness in God, our Good Father with fear and trembling, awe and wonder, covered in abundant love and mercy

Proverbs 1:7 tells us that the fear of God—Jehovah, Existing One—is the beginning of knowledge, which leads to wisdom, cunning, direction, clarity.

Then, Habakkuk 2:14 declares that the earth will be filled with the knowledge of the glory of the Lord. That knowledge is *yada* knowledge—a deep well of experiential knowing and discerning. We won't just know in our head the depth of God's glory; we will experience it. And, side note, it's an experiential knowledge of both God's wrath/righteousness and His love and mercy. See how that goes? That both/and tension again!

So, to paraphrase: Fear, reverence of Jehovah (Existing One), is the chief point, the starting point, of wisdom, cunning, maneuvering around the world while experiencing who is the One to worship and set higher than our own passions and desires—our idols. The Existing One defines what is wisdom, what is knowledge, what is worthy. Seeing Him rightly is the utmost, highest pursuit because in His glory, God defines what is good and true, righteous and worthy, delightful and fulfilling. In light of the glory, we see the face of Jesus. This is where the New Testament lens comes in to enrich Proverbs 1:7 and Habakkuk 2:14.

> For God, who said, "Let light shine out of darkness," has shone in our hearts to give the light of the knowledge of the glory of God in the face of Jesus Christ. (2 Corinthians 4:6)

We covered this in day one of this chapter but I could shout it from the rooftops and say it again:

> *Let this be what consumes us rather than those glittery idols: May the whole earth be filled with the knowledge of the glory of God, in the face of Christ Jesus, by the overflowing power of the Holy Spirit.*

Fear of the Lord is an understanding that the search for knowledge spans more than wisdom and direction. A human desires to know and *be known*. To doubt God's goodness is to seek for that which you think He is holding out on you. Sin and idolatry go hand in hand. Sin being the act of turning away from that which displeases God. Idolatry holds up things or people because we don't see God rightly.

Idolatry in modern Western terms is sneakier than the obvious abomination of the Israelites' creating the statue in the shape of a calf to worship and bow low to out of the wealth they gained from leaving Egypt (their captors) by the power of God. Yes, a golden calf is quite obvious idolatry.

A. W. Tozer speaks of idolatry: "Wrong ideas about God are the only fountain from which the polluted waters of idolatry flow; they are themselves idolatrous." He then goes on to say, "Let us beware lest we, in our pride, accept the erroneous notion that idolatry consists only in kneeling before visible objects of adoration, and that civilized peoples are therefore free from it. The essence of idolatry is the entertainment of thoughts about God that are unworthy of Him."[1]

> For although they knew God, they neither glorified Him as God nor gave thanks to Him, but their thinking became futile and their foolish hearts were darkened . . . and exchanged the glory of the immortal God for images resembling mortal man and birds and animals and creeping things. (Romans 1:21,23)

The journey of seeking, grasping, elevating on pedestals is a similar act of pursuing knowledge. To be seen, known, to know, and to be fulfilled is behind the pursuit and elevating of anything that isn't God Himself. But it's easier to grab hold of something or someone who seemingly meets our need (albeit in a temporary way) than to pursue the fulfilling knowledge of God Himself. Idols are sneaky that way. The things we can physically touch with our hands give us only an illusion of being known or satisfied. Thus, the illusion takes us into those dark places described in Romans 1 because the allure is a false light of knowledge, not the One True Light.

---

[1] *The Knowledge of Holy*, https://www.cmalliance.org/devotions/tozer?id=1301

Want to swim in the freedom of hands unclenched from worship and clinging to that which only glitters? Live in that both/and tension we talked about in day one. Why is God worthy of worship of Him and Him alone?

He is the One and Only. The UnCreated One. The Glorious One. The One who was and is and is to come. The One who will never leave or forsake us. The One who won't be held on a temporary pedestal.

And. In the light of His glory, we see the face of Jesus. To please God and worship Him only is to live in His best for His creation. Jehovah—Existing One (not the idol!)—commands us to worship only Him out of purest love and for our own good. Remember, what we perceive as the no's in God's Word are really a divine invitation to say yes to God's more and better. Idols pale in comparison to God's more and better!

I sat in His presence for months and months without typing any words or creating anything but art with my stash of watercolors and acrylics, and in those months, I let God strip away, cut back, refine, dig deeper, heal, build back, lay foundations. It was months and months of this. As excruciating as it was to not produce or create anything regarding my work, that de-throning of idols positioned me in more beautiful, Highest Pursuits of God Himself—not in what I could achieve or hold up in success.

The Lord held my heart so tenderly as He did that deep work, layer by layer. And it was good.

Grab your journal, pen, and Bible.

In your day one journal prompts, we covered God's wrath and righteousness paired with the light of God's glory in the face of Jesus. Because of the cross we have access to God Himself. Reread and write out each of these verses by way of interacting with the scriptures in a fresh way: Habakkuk 2:14; 2 Corinthians 4:6; Romans 1:21-23.

How do idols (things we hold tight and dear, things we elevate instead of God Himself) bump up against these verses?

Why does the lesser pursuit of being seen and known and to know lead us to the worship of idols?

What empty spaces do you have in your soul that tempt you to fill them with the knowledge of anything other than your loving Father?

Go ahead and name those idols. It will be hard. Just like the Lord had to give me a holy hammer to smash them, He also held me tightly and kindly as I laid down those glittery pursuits.

HIGHER PURSUIT: FEAR OF GOD (AWE & WONDER)

Journal it out

Lord, here are the things that turn my attention and affection from you...

Lord, show me Your glory. I want to know more of who You are...

Show me, Father, how to worship You alone...

DAY 3: NAME OF GOD: ADONAI

"To see Him rightly"—that is a phrase and a prayer I find rolling around in my head as I search the Word and as I create space for revival and awakening to God's fullness. Seems like a tall order. And yes, every Higher Pursuit is a tall order—difficult to pursue on our own without the guidance of the Wonderful Counselor—the Holy Spirit. What tends to happen as I journey to see Him rightly is that I remember ways I've done the whole rock-star/screaming-girl thing for a human being as if Jesus Himself walked into the room. And it is cringeworthy.

I will never, ever live this moment down. I will be ninety years old and my son will still give his dear old mom a hard time about it. My hands are shaking typing this out because this was not a proud moment by far.

You see, I live in Texas, and in Texas, football is king. In addition, I live in the same town where my husband and I went to college. Aggie Football holds a special place in my heart, for there were many dates with my once-boyfriend/now-husband where we cheered on our team together. And after we moved back to Texas and the Lord stripped away so much from my identity (in His goodness), Saturday night football with my husband and son was a balm to my soul. I wasn't achieving, but I sure was building memories with my guys!

I got caught up in a moment I'm not proud of. A local football celebrity stood for hard work, grit, sweat, winning, and lots of fun for our family. We loved Gilly. When it was his time to graduate, we were able to grab a much-coveted pic with the 12th Man of Texas A&M. As I posed my adorable 11-year-old son and grabbed my phone to snap a pic, I started squealing like a school girl. It was all I could do not to jump in on the selfie myself. Complimenting and showing gratitude for this football player's influence and delight in our life doesn't even express the level of gushing and the elevated pitch in my voice. My son gladly took the picture with our local hero and my husband just rolled his eyes in the background.

Bless.

Let me tell you, there was much repentance for my cringeworthy behavior.

I see now and I truly knew then where this moment of utter worship of a human stands in very stark contrast to the Higher Pursuit of fear of God and worshiping Him as Adonai—Master, LORD, One and Only. Let these two passages sit on your soul as you meditate on this name of God: Adonai. In these scriptures, the name *Adonai* is specifically used for a reason. Don't skim, but sit with these descriptives to read through the lens of God as Master.

> O Lord, our **Lord [Adonai]**, how majestic is your name in all the earth! You have set your glory above the heavens. Out of the mouth of babies and infants, you have established strength because of your foes, to still the enemy and the avenger. When I look at your heavens, the work of your fingers, the moon and the stars, which you have set in place, what is man that you are mindful of him, and the son of man that you care for him? (Psalm 8:1-4, emphasis mine)

> Behold, the **Lord [Adonai]** God comes with might, and his arm rules for him; behold, his reward is with him, and his recompense before him. He will tend his flock like a shepherd; he will gather the lambs in

> his arms; he will carry them in his bosom, and gently lead those that are with young. (Isaiah 40:10-11, emphasis mine)

This definition of Adonai—Master, Sovereign One, Owner—will most likely rub up against many of us at first. It feels weird to think of anything as our owner, and it almost feels antithetical to the notion of freedom that we certainly desire based on God's Word. But might we just be looking at this name of God through the lens of worldly, humanistic history and instances that are separate from the truth of who God is? I think so. To be owned by someone in our natural thinking is to be manipulated, locked up, boxed in, trapped. To be *owned by God* in our Spirit-filled, Higher Pursuit journey is to be covered, hemmed in, hidden, cared for, provided for by a loving God who lives outside of any sinful behaviors we see in earthly owners. So, to see Him rightly and to live in the fullness of Adonai, our Master, our Owner, let's go ahead and walk in faith and live out truth and trust that our human understanding will follow once we see for ourselves the fruit of following Adonai.

Sweet surrender; sacrifice of praise; see Him rightly—all three of these serve as hard and holy heart postures to take and require the Holy Spirit to propel us to our knees in humility and to lift our hands in praise.

Sweet Surrender

To learn that surrender is a gift when paired with the cross of Christ. The word "surrender" is often synonymous with weakness. But don't we know the divine paradox in the Bible! In weakness and in surrender—the letting go of our rights and privileges—there is a beautiful exchange. Jesus, whom we call Lord, who is God, Adonai, Master in the flesh, calls us to die to ourselves and follow Him in Matthew 16:24.

As the Master who leads us toward the bigger, glorious picture of the Kingdom, we find a life in communion and fellowship with the One True God.

It takes death and denial and forsaking to pick up a life abundant. This is antithetical to our human understanding that it takes straight-up, pure faith to let go. It takes an indwelling of the Spirit to surrender—a sweet surrender, in fact.

See Him Rightly

Now that we've moved to a place of un-gripping that which tethers us to the world and not to eternity, we position ourselves to see Him rightly, to see Adonai through the lens of a surrender to His perfect love and His perfect holiness.

He is God and we are not.

> …All things created by Jesus and for Jesus. (Colossians 1:16)

The first and second chapters of Colossians help us to grasp the preeminence of Christ. This big, important, weighty word tells us that Jesus is the Alpha and Omega, the beginning and the end, the One and only to whom we bow low and raise up in praise. Again, simply put: He is God and we are not.

We are not the center of the story. Jesus is. Yet we are still beloved and He calls us His.

The light of God's glory and presence shines in and informs our identity and purpose—not the other way around.

In humility and surrender, when we bow low to Jesus, Lord, Master, Adonai, this is not a degrading posture. It's one of dignity because of the One who owns us, paid for us, redeemed us.

To see Him rightly is to frame the world in God's limitless love, mercy, righteousness, power, kindness, goodness. It takes diligence and intention on our part though. We must grab an eraser and brush away the lines we've drawn and the boxes we've created with our human-limited perception of God's character and nature. Into sweet surrender and with Spirit-led eyes to see Him rightly, this is a divine invitation. Will you say yes?

Sacrifice of Praise

In another divine, circular motion, a sacrifice of praise brings us back from that which is death and into life. To sacrifice means something has to die. Something must be stripped away or relieved of its power and hold on us.

> Through him [Jesus] then let us continually offer up a sacrifice of praise to God, that is, the fruit of lips that acknowledge his name. (Hebrews 13:15)

A sacrifice costs something. The great price was paid by Jesus on the cross. The author of Hebrews tells us to continually offer a sacrifice of praise, to daily (even moment by moment) come before the altar that is the cross and die of our self and to lift up the name of Jesus alone.

To make His name the focus of our praise and attention brings a pure and good sacrifice that then leads us into the fullness of God. When in worship of Jesus, we sacrifice our idols. The smoke of that sacrifice and death on the altar of our idols is a sweet incense. To praise the One and Only is to forsake, let die, all lesser things. Our Higher Pursuit is then to offer a sacrifice of praise even when we don't "feel" like it. To let die our emotions, temporal needs, and self-focused mindsets all for the sake of choosing Christ to worship only—this is a sacrifice of praise. And it is good. And He is worthy! Instead of offering attention to our idols, let's offer an even better praise. The Word says that God is an all-consuming fire. The One who burns with love and mercy yet righteousness, bore our sins on the cross to be consumed by the fire of judgment on the sickness of sin.

He is worthy of our sacrifice and surrender to let die anything that does not lead us back to Him.

Grab a journal and these scriptures to work through your sweet surrender, seeing Him rightly, and your sacrifice of praise.

Read Psalm 8 and Isaiah 40, keeping in mind the name of God, *Adonai*—Master. For each passage, journal out these questions:

What characteristics of God are illustrated in these verses?

What is the Holy Spirit prompting you to "die to" in surrender as you read?

To see Him rightly (based on this scripture) is to do what?

HIGHER PURSUITS

With words straight from the verses you just read, write out prayers of praise to your Adonai.

What cost do you see in the act of surrender and praise? Are you propelled toward paying the price or are you compelled to shrink back? Why or why not? Hash it out with the Holy Spirit on the pages of your journal.

DAY 4: SPIRITUAL DISCIPLINE: CONFESSION AND REPENTANCE

Repentance is a beautiful thing. Some find the word old school or too churchy to wrap their mind around. This is because too many preachers have associated this spiritual discipline of repentance with fire and brimstone. But in reality, the call from Jesus Himself in Matthew 3:2 to repent is yet another divine invitation into the fullness of God and His perfect love and will for His children.

Many Old Testament scriptures called Israel to turn from their wicked ways. Second Chronicles 7:14 is a cry for Israel to turn back from her One True God and worship Adonai alone. It also serves as a revival rally cry for us as New Testament believers to get real about sin and our wicked ways.

> . . . if my people who are called by my name humble themselves, and pray and seek my face and turn from their wicked ways, then I will hear from heaven and will forgive their sin and heal their land. (2 Chronicles 7:14)

This is pretty harsh language that even reminds me of fire and brimstone. That is until I reframe the concept. My actions and thoughts in light of God's glory and holiness fall short. Way short. Without the cross of Christ, without His shed blood, without His victory over death, my sickness of sin is, in fact, wicked.

But you and I are not called to stay there and wallow in shame and sorrow for our sin. As followers of Jesus, we are called in His righteousness and empowered by His Spirit to live, really *live*, in God's love and forgiveness that redeem us back to His presence.

The Bible isn't simply a book full of no's or "you can't" but rather an invitation to God's better and best.

Does this sit well on your heart today? I hope it does. Because when we sit with the Word and read it through the lens of God's more and better for the world—for us personally—then we flip the script on how we interact with the Father. He is *holy* and perfect. He is full of life. What we perceive as a no or "you can't" is really an invitation to relationship and His best. I could preach all day long but instead I will drop in this scripture that we covered back in chapter 1.

> The Lord is my chosen portion and my cup; you hold my lot. The lines have fallen for me in pleasant places; indeed, I have a beautiful inheritance. (Psalm 16:5-6)

We read in John 4 the account of Jesus with the Samaritan woman at the well, a sinner just like you and me. A woman weary from carrying water that her life depended on, she reaped the social consequences of her sin. But when others shamed and shunned her, Jesus met the talk of her sin with His living water of life and love.

Jesus spoke of the water that only quenched her weary body and then offered her a heavenly alternative:

> Jesus said to her, "Everyone who drinks of this water will be thirsty again, but whoever drinks of the water that I will give him will never be thirsty again. The water that I will give him will become in him a spring of water welling up to eternal life."

> The woman said to him, "Sir, give me this water, so that I will not be thirsty or have to come here to draw water."

On this side of heaven, none of us will every comprehend the depth of this living water we are called to. It's beautiful to read of the woman's willingness to accept Jesus' offer in faith. Jesus kept pressing in regardless of her lack of understanding. I'm grateful for that patience myself!

We then read that Jesus uses a prophetic word of knowledge as He mentions her many husbands. At the same time, He reveals His knowledge of her lifestyle of sin as a woman who sleeps with men that are not her husband.

What's so fascinating is that we then read that the woman allows Jesus to call out her sin. Maybe she is used to this chastisement? Or maybe she senses the love and kindness yet firm hand Jesus operates in. Do you see what Jesus offers instead? A life in which she worships the One True God. For in this lifestyle of worship in spirit and in truth, the Spirit of the living God covers her. Guilt and shame are not her story. To live as a vessel of His power and love—that would be her story.

And repentance was the first page in the new chapter of her life.

We read that the woman left the well to go and tell about this man who called out her sin and offered a better way. Through this confession of her sin and the proclamation of Jesus, many then believed and turned to Him. A ripple effect happens when we choose living water offered by God's grace instead of a stagnant, stale life full of sin and un-repentance.

God offers His best in the living water that is Jesus. It's not about rules to follow or boxes to tick before you are good enough. God's best is found when we turn away from anything that tells us God is not enough, that He is holding out on us.

That churchy word you might be afraid of, "repentance," is simply described as turning away from that which displeases God and turning toward God Himself—God's best. Those ways we displease God are separation points from closeness and communion with the Lover of our Soul. Repentance is recognizing the sin, lamenting of the separation, and making an active choice to not just turn away from that sin but to turn toward God instead.

Because isn't that why we indulge in what leads to the sickness of sin? At the moment of feeling depleted and in that tipping point of distrusting God's goodness, we step into the trap and illusions of sin. And in that trap, we deny God's perfect love by picking up what we only think will fill our emptiness.

I don't want to be separated from God. I don't want *you* to be separated from Him either—not one inch in the span of this lifetime or in the length of eternity.

What if the most loving thing we could do for ourselves and for others is to get real about sin? What if the most loving thing we could do is to talk about what keeps us from the fullness of our loving God? Glossing over sin is glossing over grace. Glossing over grace is a slap in the face of the One who died to bring us back to what God originally intended for His beloved creation.

Covered in abundant love and by going so low in humility, it's time to get real about sin. It's time to stop twisting and manipulating God's Word. The Bible is very clear about what God says separates us from

Him, from His fullness, from His mercy, from His abundant love, from His forgiveness.

But do we hold God Himself in value and high regard?

My fear is that we don't—not even the Church. We don't fear separation. We don't fear wrath. We don't value righteousness and holiness, which is God's nature and what He values.

So much is at stake. It's not time to play. And it's not too late. It's time to get real about sin. Because Jesus changes everything.

To repent: turn away from what is not God's best and turn toward and fall into His loving arms as Father. Healing, restoration, mercy, joy, peace, love, forgiveness—this is God's best, which is found in the awakening of God's wonder and His victory over the sin which brings death.

Get real and confess.

Go low in your need for a savior.

Turn from death and darkness.

Turn toward God's best. Let Him speak life and light over you.

Awaken to the wonder of His glory.

Live full in His Spirit of power and love.

Dip from the deep well of the living water.

Grab your pen and Bible to work through these journal/prayer points:

Use these prayer starters to lead you into a time of confession and repentance.

Father, I come before You knowing Your love but knowing Your holiness too. I confess...

Show me, Lord, how to turn from my sin and turn toward You...

Remind me, Lord: What is Your best?

If we are to make anything about the Bible about ourselves, let it be a good hard look at our personal sin to lead us to repentance.

DAY 5: EVERYDAY REVIVAL: CLARITY—TO DULL THE SHINE OF LESSER PURSUITS

What I'm about to dive into might step on your toes a bit. And I'm okay with that. If it hurts for a second—if it peels back old thought processes to lead you to Higher Pursuits—that is mission accomplished in my mind.

I see way too many Christian women posting on social media and living a personal quest for purpose. And I'm afraid this mentality of seeking out life purpose and vision and clarity to the point of obsession has, in fact, become an idol. If we get real, the quest for purpose and vision in life only offers us a moving, unattainable target. In the process of relying on our self, our goal-minded flesh fails us the moment burnout hits and especially the moment we face inevitable failure.

To feed our idol of purpose and vision in life, this often quoted and very Insta-worthy scripture is used like a balm on our soul when seeking hope in our purpose and dreams to come to fruition:

> And we know that for those who love God all things work together for good, for those who are called according to his purpose. (Romans 8:28)

But since we have committed ourselves to Higher Pursuits, let's shake things up a bit, shall we?

The rich, deep context of that often misappropriated scripture is one of God's glory and the pursuit of becoming like Christ, conformed and surrendered to His lordship, image, ultimate plans for creation. And this is delightful. To get out of our self-focused pursuits and to take part in the grander narrative of the Kingdom is to partake in God's glory, which will never leave us bored or lacking in direction and vision for life. That which works together for good in Romans 8:28 is not the success markers of our vision board or personal mission statement. "For good" is actually the greater pleasure and delight in being conformed to the image of Jesus.

All things work together for our good to conform us, to mold us, to bring us into the greater glory that is the image of Christ—in everything we do.

That is the end goal.

He is our prize and our reward.

Our goals and dreams are most fulfilling and fruitful when the "success marker" is if we center our lives around Christ. The Holy Spirit is the One who leads us to this divine pursuit of partnering with the Kingdom instead of forging our own path.

Hopes, dreams, vision casting should fall drastically down the line of priority when this "working for our good" desire of fellowship, communion with God Himself, is the end point to look toward. It's a pursuit for sure and I love how, in 2 Corinthians 3, Paul talks about the freedom found when we hope for and behold the glory of God Himself. It's an exciting life of going deeper in the knowledge of who God is, one of "glory to glory" that we will never tire or grow bored of. Some of us are the type to jump from pursuit to pursuit, project to project, next great thing to next great thing. In the Higher Pursuit of glory to glory, we are always fruitful and fulfilled.

Our purpose is to love God with our whole heart, soul, mind, and strength and to love our neighbor as ourselves (see Matthew 22:36-40). I love a good list and this list of how to holistically go about life gives me clarity in making decisions in my job, family, relationships, finances—even my journey toward health and fitness. I often hear from women about prayer requests for direction and clarity. And in those conversations and ensuing prayer time, I pray for these women to find direction and clarity by taking the narrow road—walking through the narrow gate that is surrender to Jesus as LORD, Adonai, the only One worthy of worship and affection.

Clarity

Clarity is to see Him rightly. To see Him rightly is the Higher Pursuit that will dull the shiny,

distracting light of idols that leave us unfulfilled.

In Exodus we read that Moses chose the Higher Pursuit when he trekked up the mountain to seek God Himself. A pivotal bi-product of His time on Mount Sinai was direction and vision for Israel. Tragically, at the same time Moses was pouring himself out before Adonai on that mountain, Israel was crafting gold calfs at the base of the mountain to worship in order to serve their boredom and uncertainty. In their lesser pursuits, Israel created idols while Moses sat in the presence of God Himself. An abomination for sure!

Yes, Moses was the chosen priest to go before the glory, the weightiness of the presence of God. Israel was also the chosen people set apart, and they failed miserably. First Peter 2:9 tells us that you and I are also called the "chosen-royal priesthood" because of Jesus who made the way for us to enter into full communion with the God of the universe. Fullness in His presence is our greatest delight, although it is so very often missed in the hustle culture that is even found in the Church.

To see Him rightly—to find clarity— is to seek all of who God is, to the point of a holy obsession. To seek all of God's nature and character is to access God's glory. That light of the glory of God then shines in to inform our purpose, identity, path forward. It can't be the other way around. We can't start with "Tell me more about me, Lord." If we are to walk as women who follow Jesus and who hold His Word with reverence by the power of the Holy Spirit, if we are women who desire God's fullness, then we must look at His Word rightly to see Him rightly. Nowhere in Scripture does it tell us to seek our purpose outside of loving God with our heart, soul, mind, strength. Because, while God does use our gifts and talents for His Kingdom, those purpose mindsets and pursuits will suck us dry if our greatest reward is not simply more of God Himself.

This Kingdom clarity leads to that transformation mentioned in Romans 8:28-29. That is the goal of life, the end point: transformation toward Christ-likeness rearranges our purpose. Wasn't it Jesus who said He was about His Father's business? Yes, yes, it was!

That is clarity right there.

To see God rightly as our Highest Pursuit arranges our to-do list, agenda, life purpose, and dreams. At the end of any given day, if you forsook the hustle and simply sat in the presence of God in worship and in prayer—girl, that's a *win*. Every square inch of our lives is effected when the priority is loving God and walking on the narrow road to see Him rightly. Every square inch of our lives is enriched with glory to glory depth when the first choice is to ask God, "Tell me more of who *You* are!" You don't have to worry about being fulfilled, because Christ promises a life abundant and full for those who surrender their own agenda and follow Him.

Grab your Bible and journal:

Idols crashing down and seeing God rightly—these bring clarity to your everyday. Use these scriptures and this quote to write out a prayer full of confession, repentance, and worship of the Lord. *This is your Higher Pursuit.*

We are demolishing arguments and ideas, every high-and-mighty philosophy that pits itself against the knowledge of the one true God. We are taking prisoners of every thought, every emotion, and subduing them into obedience to the Anointed One. (2 Corinthians 10:5, The Voice)

For now, we can only see a dim and blurry picture of things, as when we stare into polished metal. I realize that everything I know is only part of the big picture. But one day, when Jesus arrives, we will see clearly, face-to-face. In that day, I will fully know just as I have been wholly known by God. (1 Corinthians 13:12, The Voice)

The streets of gold will have small attraction to us, the harps of angels will but slightly enchant us, compared with the King in the midst of the throne. He it is who shall rivet our gaze, absorb our thoughts, enchain our affection, and move all our sacred passions to their highest pitch of celestial ardour. We shall see Jesus. (Charles Spurgeon)

CHAPTER 3

HIGHER PURSUIT: BIBLICAL WORLDVIEW

DAY 1: TO FRAME TRUTH RIGHTLY

The world is full of ideologies. There are spiritual, dark forces manipulating more than we can even fathom. With sanctified eyes and a determination for spiritual discernment, we don't have to fall into the traps of that very real and present darkness.

Biblical worldview frames our perspective with absolute truth and speaks to what is happening in our world through a godly, Spirit-led lens. The phrase "absolute truth" might make some people roll their eyes, insinuating it's an outdated notion. This posture of denying absolute truth leads to wishy-washy behavior which causes one to sway to and from truth at the whim of emotion and deception caused by the works of the enemy.

When Jesus spoke of the mandate to build our houses on solid foundations—my goodness, was there ever a time in history when this truth applies?!

> And everyone who hears these words of mine and does

> not do them will be like a foolish man who built his house on the sand. And the rain fell, and the floods came, and the winds blew and beat against that house, and it fell, and great was the fall of it. (Matthew 7:24-26)

A culture that now operates in anti-God mandates will sway and topple even the best laid foundations if not centered on a biblical worldview. Biblical worldview is simply an understanding of who God is, His plan for the world, what His Word says, and how we are to live that out.

I remember sitting in an intense discipleship program where I was the youngest in the room and the least mature in my faith. There was so much room for growth and I was ready to stretch. I thought I had the concepts of the Bible down pat until I heard this one quote that sums up everything. This is not an attempt to be hyperbolic or dramatic. It truly sums up life. And, outside of Scripture, this quote and understanding about God and His creation has, hands-down, changed me and shaped me. You will see this quote in every book I write; it's that important to me.

> There's not one square inch of the entire universe where Christ, who is sovereign above all, does not claim, 'Mine.'
> (Abraham Kuyper, Dutch theologian)

And after hearing this quote spoken over the room, the Spirit flipped a switch in my understanding. Boxes around my relationship with God were busted. There's no separation, no line drawn, no square inch of creation where God does not have His sovereign hand. He moves in charge of it all.

You came to this book for Higher Pursuits while standing on the foundation of the gospel as the center point. So, let's look at a set of questions that many—even non-believers—ponder. These questions need to be asked especially when you scroll through your phone to see chaos, hatred, evil spinning out. We question internally, and many create non-profits, social-justice movements, even ministries to answer and act upon these questions:

>Where did we come from?
>What went wrong with the world?
>How do we fix it?

Without a biblical worldview, these questions are never truly answered, and solutions toward the problem serve as only a band-aid. But the Bible gives us more rich and truth-filled questions and answers:

>What did God intend? Creation
>What went wrong? Sin/the fall
>What is the solution? The cross of Christ and His resurrection (redemption)
>How do we respond? Reformation/restoration

While we will not cover the great expanse that is biblical worldview, I want us to dip our toes in together and wade for just a bit. There are a handful of trusted resources I will offer you at the end of this chapter. We will cover four main themes in Scripture that have played out in the history of time: creation, the fall, redemption, restoration. As one who loves a good list to help me make sense of just about anything, these themes do my soul good when I'm sifting through everything from relationships to what I see in my news feed. Remember, the phrase "biblical worldview" starts with the assumption that the Bible is God's authoritative and inerrant word. What He says and who He says He is will be found in Scripture, and if you look through this worldview lens of themes and are led by the Holy Spirit, the flow of how we see human history comes alive. It's not just elusive concepts in the dusty front half of your Bible!

Let's start with Creation.

The questions—Who is God? Where did the world come from? Who am I?—all lead us back to Genesis 1 and 2. If you grew up in church, your perception of Genesis might be swayed by cute little cartoon characters telling you the story of creation. Don't let that well-meaning attempt to capture the attention of kids water down the gritty, powerful, and unfathomable story of how it all started. What we can't fathom with our human-limited understanding leaves room for the Spirit of the living God to blow up our imagination us as we read His Word and study creation through science and the tangible evidence of a Divine Creator.

Let these verses simmer on your soul:

> At first the earth lacked shape and was totally empty, and a dark fog draped over the deep while God's spirit-wind hovered over the surface of the empty waters. Then there was the voice of God. (Genesis 1:2, The Voice)

> God saw that the light was beautiful and good, and He separated the light from the darkness. (Genesis 1:4, The Voice)

> So God parted the waters and formed this expanse, separating the waters above from the waters below. It happened just as God said. (Genesis 1:7, The Voice)
> God called the dry land "earth" and the waters congre-

gated below "seas." And God saw that His new creation was beautiful and good. (Genesis 1:10)

Lights, come out! Shine in the vast expanse of heavens' sky dividing day from night to mark the seasons, days, and years. Lights, warm the earth with your light. It happened just as God said. (Genesis 1:14-15)

God made earth-creatures in a vast variety of species: wild animals, domesticated animals of all sizes, and small creeping creatures, each able to reproduce its own kind. God saw that His new creation was beautiful and good. (Genesis 1:25)

Now let Us conceive a new creation—humanity—made in Our image, fashioned according to Our likeness. And let Us grant them authority over all the earth. (Genesis 1:26)

So God did just that. He created humanity in His image, created them male and female. Then God blessed them and gave them this directive: "Be fruitful and multiply. Populate the earth. I make you trustees of My estate." (Genesis 1:27-28)

And the man and woman were both found in the Garden of Eden—a place of delight—walking with God in the cool of the day. And they were both naked and not ashamed. (Genesis 2:25; 3:8, paraphrased)

There is nothing dry or flat or cartoonish about any of this creation account. Here are some important things to remember with regards to a biblical worldview about creation:

- God the Father, God the Son, God the Holy Spirit created the universe out of nothing—with astounding precision. Fun fact: if Earth was only slightly closer to the sun, the water would boil away. If Earth was only a bit farther away from the sun, water would freeze, and our landscape would be barren. Crazy, right?

- Man and woman were created in God's image, each with distinct, God-ordained qualities that express the glory and goodness of the Lord.

- The earth was filled by God with animals, plants, water, deserts, mountains, etc., all to be kindly cared for and stewarded by man and woman.

It's important to refrain from looking at Scripture through the lens of "Tell me more about me." But it's equally important to remember that when the world is dark and spinning out, *you*, created by the Creator-God, must look to His goodness and grandeur all around you. He holds His beloved creation ever so carefully in the palm of His powerful hands. That means you too!

The Fall

What is wrong with this world? Talking about sin isn't fun. Talking about how humanity fell away from the perfect design of a good Father whose desire is to live in full communion with His beloved creation is devastating. It's especially devastating if we see things through the lens of what *could be* as we attempt to grasp the depth of what we are missing out on because of the fall: the fullness of God's presence. It's tempting to continue wallowing in the darkness as the fog causes us to forget that Jesus came to defeat it. And while we will get to reconciliation and redemption next, the conversation about sin and the fall of humanity only helps us to grow in gratitude for what Jesus did on the cross.

We read in Genesis that in the Garden of Eden—the place of true delight and fellowship—Adam and Eve fell into the trap of Satan and questioned the goodness of God. A slippery question I think we all might ask every now and then: *Did God really say . . . ?*

Doubt is not bad. Questioning is not wrong. It's when we forget about God's goodness *for us* that we slide down the slippery slope toward sin. Is God's word, what He says and commands, good for me? Is He really who He says He is? Do I believe this temptation before me will fill the void at the moment or is God's best within the confines of His commandments because He is good and kind and His ways are beautiful?

That moment we read in Genesis 3 changed everything and ushered sin into the story of man and woman through the ages.

But just what is sin? In light of cultivating a biblical worldview and seeing this greater narrative of history and of God's story, let's refresh our understanding. Sin is any action, thought, or spoken word that moves against God's perfect love, righteousness, power. Sin separates us from God's original design: His creation (man and woman) living in full fellowship, in the fullness of His glory with their Father God.

Why?

Because in His perfect holiness, God has nothing to do with the sickness of sin. But for Jesus! Because of His death on the cross and resurrection—death to life!—we are reconciled to that glorious fullness. God, in His goodness and kindness, leaves ninety-nine to go after the one (see Matthew 18:12-13). He is grieved when each and every one of us is separated from Him by sin. This is the individual fallout of the fall.

And then, there's a macro, global effect of the fall. The effects of sin and brokenness can be found in every square inch of our existence, from murder of the unborn to corruption in government. From poorly stewarding resources of the earth to human trafficking. From seemingly meaningless gossip to stealing candy from the dollar shop. God, in His goodness, allows us free will to choose Him and His best or succumb to those questions of distrust and turn our heads and hearts from Him and toward destruction. But the enemy of our soul does not have the final word and will only wreak havoc for a time predetermined by God Himself. And what was stolen will be redeemed and bought back through the cross of Christ. His resurrection from the grave defeated death, shame, guilt for our sins.

This is the beauty of the goodness of God: He knew from the beginning how His beloved would fall and He had a rescue plan.

Grab your journal, Bible, and pen.

At the risk of sounding cheesy, plan a date with God out in creation. A hike or even something as simple as taking lunch at a local park will delight your soul. With the wide-open spaces before you, crack open Genesis and read chapters 1-3. Ask the Holy Spirit to clear out any previous assumptions from reading this familiar passage.

Can you imagine the communion that Adam and Eve had with God? Does this spark a longing in your own soul for your Creator? It's okay if it doesn't. Truly. Ask Him to show you more of who He is and His desire for communion and fellowship with you.

What stirs in you when you read about the fall? Brain-dump any and all emotions or questions that you have.

What thoughts or even confusion might you have about your belief system thus far in your life? Have you come to a place where you know without a doubt, or perhaps you are leaning on the faith of a spouse, parent, friend, pastor? Hash it all out with the Lord.

DAY 2: REDEMPTION AND RESTORATION: BIG WORDS TO GRAB HOLD OF

Will you sit with this scripture for a sec?

> He [God!] has delivered us from the domain of darkness and transferred us to the kingdom of his beloved Son, in whom we have redemption, the forgiveness of sins. (Colossians 1:13-14)

We have access to the infinite glory and presence of God all because of the cross. His death makes way for you and me to walk in Christ's righteousness straight to the throne of grace (see Hebrews 4:16). Grace: God's favor, His presence surrounding you in full fellowship that was originally intended for His creation. And because of His victory over sin and death, we know the darkness has no final say; God's glory outshines the darkness. His power, love, and mercy overcome.

Jesus was the blood sacrifice for our sin. Do you grasp the weightiness of that? God placed Himself on the cross to bring us from death to life. This is a quest we should all be on: to understand God's perfect holiness, to understand His goodness, to know the gravity of our sin, to praise Jesus for the cross that redeemed us and returned us to the fullness of the Father. Let's dig into the word "redemption." With the definition of "liberation" or "deliverance through the payment of ransom," this takes us to the conversation of what exactly we need liberating from. Just as we saw in the fall, Adam and Eve and thus humanity, fell from access to God and His presence. And in that fall, all of humanity is subject to the shackles of Satan and the oppression of sin.

A high price was paid to ransom God's beloved back into righteousness—right standing—with our holy and pure Father. When God in the flesh (Jesus) came to be the sacrifice for our sin and the sins of the world, this was the greatest act of love. This is where we get back to the both/and of God we talked about in chapter 2, fear of God. In His holiness and righteousness, only the holy and righteous have access to what makes their heart, soul, spirit complete: fellowship with the Creator-God—Elohim. *But*, because this is unattainable on our own, and in His mercy and love, Jesus, *God in the flesh*, paid the blood sacrifice to ransom us (redeem) from the grips of the enemy of our soul.

> Therefore, brothers, since we have confidence to enter the holy places by the blood of Jesus, by the new and living way that he opened for us through the curtain, that is, through his flesh, and since we have a great priest over the house of God, let us draw near with a true heart in full assurance of faith, with our hearts sprinkled clean from an evil conscience and our bodies washed with pure water. (Hebrews 10:19-22)

Remember the veil? See how this all comes together? Remember that holy place we arrive at when we seek the face of God? This is the beautiful synergy of God's plan for humanity and the lens we get to look through to make sense of the world.

There's a lot to talk about with the words "freedom" and "liberation." As they imply, there is in fact oppression. While many in the world decry oppression, and while people and systems are evil and oppressive, to ignore the ultimate arbiter of slavery is to give Satan more room to have his way on the earth. Restoration is what's called for next as we look at the mandate to live as those set free, carrying the good news of true freedom.

But before we start the fun talk of the "doing" in the act of restoration living, feel a fresh wave of gratitude by way of sitting in worship of our Yeshua—Jesus—our Great High Priest.

> Thank You, Jesus,
> the new and living way,
> our Redeemer,
> our narrow gate into God's presence,
> the One in whom we are forgiven and set free.

My Redeemer lives!

Restoration. Reformation.

The divine act of reconciliation through the blood shed by Christ brings a call for those surrendered to the power, mercy, lordship of Christ to bring the ministry of reconciliation into every square inch.

> Therefore, if anyone is in Christ, he is a new creation. The old has passed away; behold, the new has come. All this is from God, who through Christ reconciled us to himself and gave us the ministry of reconciliation; that is, in Christ God was reconciling the world to himself, not counting their trespasses against them, and entrusting to us the message of reconciliation. Therefore, we are ambassadors for Christ. (2 Corinthians 5:18-20)

When Jesus taught the disciples to pray, "Your Kingdom come," when He commanded His followers to go and tell of this Kingdom and make disciples, and when He preached about living as a light in the darkness and as salt that preserves the earth from corruption—this was the command for reconciliation, restoration, reformation.

Bringing others into relationship with their good Father; moving in the God-created world around you to restore and renew—this is what it looks like this side of the cross of Christ.

As new creations in Christ, we have the directive to partner with heaven to first pray, then seek, reform, and transform our world to see the goodness of heaven make things right in the world. As new creations in Christ, filled with wisdom by the power of the Holy Spirit, might our higher pursuit be to look at problems in the world and ask Him first for divinely inspired solutions? Spirit-led creation—of art, media, accounting, parenting, teaching, engineering, medical care, leadership, governing, etc.—brings beauty and restoration. The Bible is our framework; the blood of Christ is our salvation from sin and darkness; the direction and clarity from the Holy Spirit offer creative solutions. All of this to the glory and honor of our Creator-God, Elohim.

This seems like a daunting task. It's also mind-boggling to live in the tension of holding faith for restoration in the present and in the ultimate fulfillment of redemption, restoration, reconciliation when Jesus comes again. Romans 8 tells us that creation groans and eagerly awaits to be set free from the effects of sin that began at the fall. Even creation, not only humans, show effects of deprivation that comes because of sin. But because Jesus died and rose again to defeat that corruption, we get to work alongside God to restore creation with gospel-redeeming, good-news transforming solutions inspired by the Spirit of the living God.

You are a new creation, you strive to live surrendered to the Lord, you have the mind of Christ, and you seek His face in awe and wonder—fear. What, then, is He beckoning you to restore in your sphere of influence? Take one square inch at a time. Every small act of obedience is seen by Jesus as an act of love. Remember how He said, "If you love Me, you will keep My commands" (John 14:15)?

Bring beauty. Bring mercy. Bring forgiveness. Bring Spirit-filled solutions. Bring justice. Plead the blood of Jesus over sin, darkness, and corruption. Create. Innovate. Pray like never before. Be bold. Be generous. Speak truth.

Bring restoration—one square inch at a time.

Let's put pen to paper. Grab your Bible and journal.

Review the quote by Abraham Kuyper on day one. Make a list of your "every square inch"—for example: family, friendships, work, finances, ministry, hobbies. Let's look at each of these areas in light of biblical worldview/restoration. Start brainstorming some ways you can bring biblical concepts and mandates into these square inches. For example, we are called to be generous (see 2 Corinthians 9:6-8). What would this look like in regards to your finances and giving? Keep this list on hand all week and add to it throughout your day.

DAY 3: NAME OF GOD: ELOHIM—STRAIGHT TO THE SOURCE

Elohim, the name of God used in Genesis—the beginning. To worship God as Elohim is to recognize and give honor to the All Powerful One—Creator.

The Creator—the Uncreated One.

Did you catch that? None before Him and none after Him and the only one who created every molecule of your being. In a world where we can Google any answer that suits our belief, and in a world where statements like "that's my truth" shun finite, absolute statements, there is One who created all—and He is *good*. These would be fighting words to anyone not willing to lay down ego and control.

But we must make an even more finite, absolute statement regarding the God of the Bible, because those who throw around New Age statements like "that's my truth" don't bat an eye at the use of the word "god," for they create little gods in their own image all day long. And to get real and raw about it, it's not just New Agers guilty of this! We've confronted our own man-made idols in our Higher Pursuit of the fear of God alone, right? Yes!

But to find yourself on solid ground rather than on a wishy-washy worldview is to go straight to the source.

I started brainwashing my kid at a young age—anything from "don't touch the hot stovetop" as a toddler to "be quick to forgive and pray for the bully at school" to "if you really want to know the truth about things like sex, listen to me and not ignorant sixth-graders who know nothing." Why? How do I know? *Because I'm Mom and I'm awesomely smart.* And, welp, he might roll his eyes and say, "Because you are Mom and you are awesomely smart," but he does, in fact, come to me and his father for firsthand information. I have shamelessly brainwashed my kid to come to us with anything and everything if he wants to know the real truth. Straight to the source. This illustration does, however, fall short due to the sheer fact that the God of the universe—Creator, Elohim, the Original Source—doesn't need to manipulate to position Himself in authority.

The intricacies of the universe point to a divine being—God, the Uncreated One. The spinning out of sin and darkness point to the need for a Savior. And the search to make sense of the world is found when led by the Spirit of revelation—that is, the Holy Spirit, Wonderful Counselor.

We see Elohim praised as all-powerful Creator all over the Old Testament and especially in the psalms. What's fascinating is the depth of understanding given the limited science and technology available in ancient days. So with simple yet powerful faith, let's step into the world of Old Testament worship of Elohim.

Grab your journal and Bible.

What have you learned about creation from school or Google that makes you question a Divine Creator? Did you know that by taking these questions to the Lord as you are led by the Holy Spirit for answers and renewed faith, you are communing with God? He can handle your doubt and questions!

What do you see in the beauty of creation that makes you delight in Elohim?

One of my best ways to ground myself when life seems swirly is to simply write out scripture. I usually head to the book of Psalms, which is a great place for us to land today in our conversation about Elohim—all-powerful Creator. Might I suggest Psalms 8, 96, and 139? Go all in and start writing out this scripture to inscribe it on your heart as a way to worship today. Bonus tip: I keep a separate notebook just for writing out the Word. We never know when the day might come when we no longer have access to our Bibles. Might a covert, seemingly meaningless composition notebook go unnoticed to those who disdain the Word of God?

DAY 4: SPIRITUAL DISCIPLINE-STUDY THE WORD

So, funny thing, as I write this book, I'm currently practicing the art of eating whole foods and cutting out junk and all things processed and packaged. I thought I was a pretty clean eater before. But it wasn't until I took a holistic look at my diet, my pantry, and what nutrition is all about that I realized I was missing out on God-given vitamins, minerals, wellness when I was eating foods that only offer empty calories and no nutrition. And as I'm typing this, I'm chuckling to myself regarding that beautiful metaphor of bread woven through the Old and New Testaments. If you've put even your pinky toe into the vast ocean of clean eating, you would know that not all carbs are created equal, and some people even put a red X over carbs as a whole!

I think it is important to note: bread and carbs that have been processed to make them quick and easy to use are the ones that no longer carry the nutritional value…the fiber and nutrients our bodies need. Likewise, when we take a quick and easy, processed, if you will, approach to Scripture, we miss out on the full nutrients…of all it has to offer us. We don't want bits of pieces of scripture. We want whole Scripture…whole food for our heart, soul, mind and strength.

I love bread, let me tell you. And the Bible is full of stories, metaphors, teachings, and provision offered in the form of bread. But to understand the rich meaning and necessity of using bread references, we need to look at the Word of God as a whole. The same goes for all of the themes of biblical worldview: creation, the fall, redemption/reconciliation, restoration/reformation. To use our modern understanding of bread, for example, is to miss out on the fullness God offers as a He weaves in themes and teachings of who He says He is. Bottom line: we must come to understand God in the fullness of His Word (by the power of the Holy Spirit). This is only achieved by consuming God's Word as a whole and as it was originally intended to be read. Far too often we take scriptures out of context. Social media memes and cute posters to decorate the walls of our homes make us feel cute and comfy with the Word of God but leave us way short of the fullness as we consume only bites and not the whole loaf—as we come to the Word with only limited understanding of context and through the lens of Western mindsets.

The book of John starts us off with an astounding verse that describes Jesus: "In the beginning, was the Word, and the Word was with God, and the Word was God." John soon ties this all-encompassing statement to Jesus: "And the Word became flesh and dwelt among us, and we have seen his glory, glory as of the only Son from the Father, full of grace and truth" (John 1:14).

Grace and truth. Grace: access to the favor and the presence of God Himself. Truth: the understanding of the nature of our Creator and His perfect plan for creation. Grace: abundant provision and love because of the cross of Christ. Truth: the firm foundation to stand on when operating by the power of the Holy Spirit to live out commands created as God's best for His creation. Jesus, in His I AM statements, declared His deity and nature as He started with "I AM the bread of life":

> I am the bread that gives life. If you come to My table and eat, you will never go hungry. Believe in Me, and you will never go thirsty. (John 6:35, The Voice)

The ways of the world leave us hungry and malnourished. Jesus satisfies our ultimate hunger and desire, which come from yearning for and knowing our Creator.

The ways of the world leave us thirsty, dry, and empty. Jesus offers rivers of living water to flow out of us in power, love, mercy through His Spirit. Stagnant lives full of apathy are not God's intention for His people.

To know this Bread of Life is to consume the whole loaf, not just crumbs or morsels. But to truly know the depth of His mercy and love for us comes with the task of digging, studying, praying, writing out, wrestling, doubting, questioning, reconciling, realigning, worshiping in grace and truth. And we have access to this full picture by the grace of truth given to us in God's Word—in the Bible. Oh how we've missed out on the fullness when we take meme-worthy scripture out of the bigger picture to fit our goals, need for success, need to be known, need to make a point, etc.

For example, something I could shout on every roof top is the mandate to live *not* just as Jeremiah 29:11 women but to live as women of Jeremiah 29:12, 13, 14, 15! Yes, to prosper, to have hope and a future is God's desire for us. But the true prize and true future are found when we seek God with our whole heart. He is our reward. God Himself! And if we really want to dig into what that often-quoted, and misquoted, scripture is about, it's smack dab in the middle of the painful story of Israel's wayward worship of idols and the ensuing captivity of the nation by Babylon. They sinned. They worshiped idols. They turned their faces from their Father. They were enslaved, killed, tortured, and kept captive for 70 years. God allowed another nation to overtake them. And, in His kindness, He offered a future in light of their despair and ultimately promised that His presence would sustain them. Kind of different from the cute way we tend to quote Jeremiah 29 in hopes of a great job, money, future, purpose, right? Sin takes us off the path God designed for us. But He is our reward and hope and He will be found when we seek Him first—seek Him with all our heart and forsake our need for prosperity and easy living.

And don't even get me started on how outraged I get when I read Instagram posts quoting Habakkuk along with someone's vision board in hopes of manifesting dreams of hustle-filled "girl boss" lives with the abundance of cash to fund said dream. In the original context of the scripture, which commands them to "write the vision on the wall," was the warning that captivity and destruction were on their way for Israel. Not cute, right? This was a different kind of vision and warning, for sure, and entirely different from the use of the Bible to motivate one to "dream big!"

So to move as women in both grace and truth and to live confident in our worldview grounded in God's Word, let's endeavor to eat the entire loaf and not be afraid to dig in. We have the Wonderful Counselor—the Holy Spirit, God in us—to lead and guide us. It's a process and a journey that doesn't start and end with a few minutes of quiet time to check the box and get on with our days. Yes, the Word in only crumbs and morsels will do us good. God is kind like that. But the Higher Pursuit is to consume the entirety, however hard and heavy, because to know God and seek His face in light of His Word is to find true hope, prosperity, a future, and satisfaction. It won't always make sense. Sometimes you will be bored. Sometimes it's mind-boggling. But when we just show up, our Bread of Life will meet us and we will be filled to the full.

Grab your Bible and journal. Let's start eating the whole loaf!

As I mentioned before, context is key. Right now we are going to take a well-known "motivational" scripture and blow things up a bit to better understand what the Lord would have for us in His Word.

> I can do all things through Christ who strengthens me.
> (Philippians 4:13)

I'm going to ask you to go ahead and read the entire book of Philippians. If this takes you a while or a couple of sittings, that's okay! Still read the whole book. And while you read, ask yourself these key Bible reading questions:

- Who wrote the book?

- Who is it written to?

- What's the historical context? (Many Bibles offer even just a paragraph or two at the introduction of each book. Don't skip yours!)

- What is the main theme?

- What is the encouragement offered?

- What commands or warnings are offered?

- What is it telling you about the nature of God?

After you read the entire book, circle back to chapter 4 and reread it. What is Philippians 4:13 hitting on? What is Paul saying about his faith and ministry? Does it bounce off of your understanding of this verse? Does it enrich your understanding of contentment, God's provision, call to a life of ministry, however the sacrifice?

In this exercise of reading scripture in context, what did you learn?

It's imperative that we take the time to consume the Word and read not just individual verses but grab hold of the themes of that whole paragraph, chapter, or book. There is value in taking time to slow down and prayerfully study, maybe even wrestle with, the whole loaf of the Word. Don't settle for just the crumbs and morsels!

DAY 5: EVERYDAY REVIVAL: A MANDATE TO SHINE BRIGHTLY

The moment was not Instagram-able. You know those times when you wish you could share it with the world but somehow grabbing your phone to stage a picture would stifle the moment of holiness? This was that and I had to fight every bit of myself to dilute the moment into a social square with a 24-hour shelf life.

We had been praying for months over our city and nation. Revival was the goal. Awakening was the hope. A move of the Holy Spirit was the mandate we were placing on heaven simply out of desperation and knowing that was our first and only option. Month after month, the hype of these prayer meetings waned and the group shrunk to fewer than ten people per meeting. And still we persisted in prayer because we knew the Lord was present and He heard our cries.

One night, the prayer points shifted to intercession for what so many have seen as an end-times harvest of souls coming soon. Multitudes coming to Jesus to surrender their lives to Him as Lord and Savior. And an awakening of the church of Christ to rise up and be filled with the Spirit of the living God. I had to rearrange my hopes and dreams for this upcoming outpouring and understand that it would probably come in the midst of even darker times than our world is in now. Many have said that in the darkness, God's glory shines brighter. This gives me hope for sure.

The prayer meeting leader then moved us into praying for the workers. We know the Word says that the harvest is plenty but the workers are few. So we prayed not just for ministers, worship leaders, or missionaries, but for anyone and everyone who handles rightly the gospel. We prayed they would make ready for the many who would encounter God in this outpouring. And as I prayed, I saw the white field symbolizing a full harvest and I felt the Lord impress upon me these poignant things to remember when this moment in history is fulfilled:

- Multitudes would have an encounter with the living God. God Himself would pour out His Spirit so that many around the globe would experience His love, power, mercy.

- Multitudes of proclaimed Christians would encounter the living God and wake up to the reality of who He is rather than the religious notions of who they only thought He was. A desire for worship in the Spirit and in truth would arise. The time to "play church" would be over.

- There would no longer be a need for celebrity Christians—if there ever really was a heavenly need for it. I think not! But because the multitudes will encounter *God Himself*, they won't need a "super Christian" to influence their faith.

- There will be a need for those who handle rightly the Word to tell the multitudes of *Who* they just encountered. This will also be a multitude of nameless, faceless, seemingly unknown people who simply love Jesus and want others to know Him and live in His fullness—thus the need for corporate prayer *now* over this group of those who will be called to disciple the multitudes.

My goodness! This is like a fire in my belly to equip you and call you into Higher Pursuits now in order to make ready for this forthcoming outpouring. And because it will most likely come in the midst of much darkness and deception, it's imperative that we know truth, that we live out a biblical worldview, and that we are filled with the Spirit of the living God so as not to be caught up in the chaos to come. Your worldview hinges on the knowledge of Jesus and who He is. It's not about a head knowledge but a holistic faith of seeking the glory of God in the face of Christ Jesus, by the power of the Holy Spirit. If I say that once in this book, I will say it a thousand times and also shout it from the rooftops!

While I prayed, I felt the Lord imploring that what He will use in this glorious upcoming season are men and women who live out of grace and truth that are Jesus Himself (see John 1:14) and are out of the overflow of a life surrendered to Him alone. But, in the meantime, I'm afraid many will miss a fruitful time of preparation by operating in lesser things rather than Higher Pursuits.

A funny distraction often bubbles up in a very well-meaning journey to find a life that counts for something. All too often I see women of all ages flat-out obsessed with finding their purpose. Social media makes it easy to think that grand actions, events, ministry, large numbers, high payouts, likes, viral videos, and more are the equivalent of God-given purpose—of God's approval. These things aren't bad at all. It's the way we see them from afar and seek to emulate in hopes of fulfilling our need to make our own life worthy and to hear the world say, "Well done." So many Christians fall into this trap when, if they read their Bibles and let the Spirit lead them, they would know to the depths of their core that the only "well done" to hear is that from Jesus Himself.

And Jesus made the conversation of purpose quite easy: to love God heart, soul, mind, strength; and to love others as yourself. This greatest commandment doesn't have to have an elaborate vision board or business plan to see it played out. A willing, surrendered heart will do just fine.

We are called to seek the fullness of God with the fullness of who He created us to be.

We are called to deny our self, pride, agenda, goals, aspirations to take up our cross and follow Him alone. This means putting to death anything that promotes self instead of the fame and renown of Jesus. This means to put to death sin and guilt that separate us from His fullness and the satisfaction found in His presence alone.

We are called to choose Jesus as the only way, truth, and life. That narrow gate and the narrow road are different from the world that calls us to live our hashtag best life, hustle, be a *boss*, follow our dreams.

All this seems like a tall order. It is. But a biblical framework simplifies the need for purpose and clarity in life. As one living this side of the cross of Christ, it's a privilege to know we get to live a life of restoration. This is all found in the knowledge that God created the world, that sin came in but has no final say, and that Jesus sacrificed Himself and shed His blood to bring us back to the original intent of fellowship/communion with our good Father. The Holy Spirit gives us power and counsel to be in the world, to love our world, and to offer Spirit-filled solutions to what is yet to be restored in light of God's goodness. We are agents of restoration because we serve the only One who truly brings reconciliation. We are ambassadors of the cross because the cross changed everything. Might we be obsessed with abiding in Christ and living out restoration through the overflow of His love? I think so. My prayer is that you will be filled with the Spirit of wisdom and revelation of God Himself with an assurance and confidence that you are loved. Then your life becomes an overflow of that at any given moment.

Might I offer a few things to consider when you find yourself without purpose, direction, or clarity?

- Stop and worship. A kingdom perspective will always do you good as you get over your self and make much of Jesus.

- Ask God who you can love and serve right in front of you, right here and now.

- Pray for the welfare of your city. Pray for revival and awakening. Pray for many to surrender their lives to Jesus. Pray for healing and miracles. Pray for the Church to be on fire with His Spirit. Then pray some more.

- Repent of any pride that this life is all about you, your dreams, your vision, your goals.

- Steward well the season you are in. What is in front of you? Stop looking for that "next thing" and sit in worship and surrender to love God and love others right where you are.

CHAPTER 4

HIGHER PURSUIT: PURSUIT OF HOLINESS

DAY 1: WITH ABANDON: DAVID

It culminated with the very king of Israel, David, dancing like a fool half-naked in the courtyard. And I can't imagine a better conclusion to a journey filled with the weighty glory of God being returned to His rightful seat in the holy city, Jerusalem, Zion, the city on a hill.

David traded his kingly robes, jewels, fine cloth and color for that of a linen ephod. A simple white garment would pale in comparison in the minds of those who value earthly symbols of status and wealth. But, in that moment of dancing, sacrifice, wild worship, David chose the garb of a priest in order to attend to the worship and sacrifice of Yahweh. What kind of king forsakes the niceties and propriety of royal stature for the humble clothing and set-apart, consecrated actions of a temple priest? As I'm typing this, I'm reminded that the ultimate King Jesus did just that when He left the splendor of heaven to be born in a dusty stable and die on a cross between two thieves. David is often seen as a type and foreshadow of Christ. You and I would do well to go by way of David as we are called to be like Christ too!

Again the question: What kind of king would choose to worship like a priest of God instead of sit on his throne? David did. He chose to minister to God in that moment. For after one beholds the glory of the living God, bold acts of consecration and honor are the only way to proceed.

And then there was this:

> As the ark of the Lord came into the city of David, Michal the daughter of Saul looked out of the window and saw King David leaping and dancing before the Lord, and she despised him in her heart. (2 Samuel 6:16)

The scorn of his wife Michal could have scorched David's ego or deterred such wild rejoicing. But he wasn't phased.

In our pursuit of holiness, many will feel the conviction for consecration yet reject it in order to protect their own ego, pride, status—sin. To behold and value God's presence and begin a lifelong journey of the pursuit of holiness will propel you to great lengths in sacrificing your life, your rights, fleshly pleasures, to pursue a holistic lifestyle that pleases the Most Holy One. And He is so good. In the pursuit and commitment to follow His Word, we see that His commands are His best for creation. It does my soul good to passionately pursue that which pleases God. I was created to align my heart, soul, mind, and body with Kingdom life and principles. To turn from sin and flesh is to walk in the fullness intended before the fall. A pursuit of holiness is to live a resurrection life toward restoration. See how that works? When we choose to view the world from a biblical lens, we will be motivated in our pursuit of holiness. When we see clearly, there is no longer space to play around in this present life once we have a clear understanding of the themes of the past and the mandates of resurrection/reconciliation/restoration this side of the cross!

Let's go back to our scene from 2 Samual 6 with David. The base dancing and wild worship all commenced with a holy yet arduous journey to bring the ark of God back to Jerusalem. Today, we have the privilege of carrying God's glory-filled presence.

Paul exhorts us in the declaration that the very bodies of Christ followers are temples of the Holy Spirit—God Himself (see 1 Corinthians 6:19). Think of that. A life filled with the passion for holiness is a life driven by the Spirit of God—the holy One. Hear me say, if you don't have this passion yet, keep going with your Higher Pursuits. The altar of your life surrendered to Jesus—this altar will be lit on fire simply with a willingness to seek His face out of awe, wonder, and reverence. Holy Spirit, will You light the flame?

We get to live on this side of the cross. Thank You, Jesus!

In King David's time, the ark of God was a holy altar in which Elohim most literally dwelt. There were important protocols and procedures to protect the purity of worship and to emphasize the holiness of the One whom they worshiped and served. David and the company of Levites journeyed to carry the ark back to Jerusalem—Zion—the City on a Holy Hill. I love the holistic nature of Scripture. Though I've read this account of the holy journey that culminated in David's radical dancing, pairing this scripture with Psalm 24 gave me richer insight and even personal application in my own pursuit of holiness.

> Who shall ascend the hill of the Lord?
>   And who shall stand in his holy place?
> He who has clean hands and a pure heart,
>   who does not lift up his soul to what is false
>   and does not swear deceitfully.

> He will receive blessing from the Lord
> > and righteousness from the God of his salvation.
>
> (Psalm 24:3-5)

David writes in this psalm a declaration of decision for those who desire to walk in the fullness of God—for those who walk in Higher Pursuits. Do you want to move and live in eternal heavenly ways? Do you want to ascend past the temporal earthly things and mindsets? Do you simply want God?

> Offer clean hands.
> Offer a pure heart.
> Keep your soul away from idols.

Jesus hits home with these same decision points in the Beatitudes. Do you want to be blessed?

> A pure heart sees God.
> A hunger and thirst for righteousness will be satisfied.

These are mile markers in our personal pursuit of holiness. These mile markers are not to be taken lightly. But they are not achieved alone. But for Jesus!

Cleansed by the blood of Jesus, we are now pure and free to see God. This doesn't negate those decision points that we must wrestle with daily. That is the pursuit of holiness—not to win grace, favor, blessing, or position with God, but to honor the holy One who is worthy. And in our acts of holiness, our life of worship calls for the gates like those poetically mentioned in Psalm 24. These are the gates of the Holy City—the place where God chose to dwell. He now dwells in *you*.

Will we be the generation of those "who seek him who seek the face of the God of Jacob" (Psalm 24:6)?

Swing wide, O Gates! Make way for the King. Make ready! He came once as the Lamb who was slain and He is coming back as the Lion with a holy roar of victory.

Grab your journal and Bible.

Look up the definition of "consecrate" and write it out. Next, journal about how this definition sits with you. Does it convict you? Does it call you higher? What is rubbing up against you with this definition? Write out a prayer about that discomfort.

What does your own pursuit of holiness look like today? There is no condemnation at all. This is just a simple place of evaluation.

Read Psalm 24 and 2 Samuel 6. Imagine the Holy Hill (God's presence) as mentioned in Psalm 24. Sit for a while in silence and ask the Holy Spirit to stir your affections and imagination. There's no right or wrong answer. Write out anything that comes to mind.

How can you offer the Lord, today, clean hands? What areas of repentance are you called to?

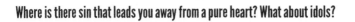

Where is there sin that leads you away from a pure heart? What about idols?

Do you see these acts of confession and repentance as worthwhile to position you to "ascend the hill of the Lord"? Ask the Lord for Spirit-led motivation to pursue holiness today.

DAY 2: JOHN THE BAPTIST: THE SUN WILL RISE

My friend quietly approached me after the meeting and whispered that she had a word for me. This kind of thing was not unusual with the crowd at that particular meeting, so I didn't bat an eye and sat excited for her to offer this prophetic word.

She simply said, "Sarah, the sun will rise. Don't be afraid of the light."

To clarify, she mentioned the word was specifically "sun" not "Son" (as in Son of God) and that she had no interpretation. Intrigued, I thanked her for her quiet obedience to listen to God's voice and share with me.

For a couple of years I sat with that prophetic word in prayerful anticipation that the Lord would illuminate it as much as it was already filled with holy illumination and talk of the sun rising and bright light. Though I didn't want to cherry-pick Scripture to confirm this word, for a long time I did keep an eye out and an ear attuned to the Holy Spirit for any time the Word stirred remembrance of this intriguing prophetic encouragement. Oftentimes, when we get a word, it is directly about our life, to encourage and comfort. And as verses such as Isaiah 60:1 were highlighted especially with regard to glory and talk of rising up, I never had peace that this "sun will rise" word was just for me personally.

Fast-forward to summer and fall of 2020. I prayed diligently and for hours about the upheaval in the world and the upcoming election in America. I prayed for holiness to prevail, for light to shine in dark crevices of corruption, to root out evil and bring it out in the open. I, of course, prayed for revival and for the Church to wake up and operate in fullness of spiritual discernment, prayer, worship, and warfare. The morning was memorable. It was a pivotal day in our country's history, and through listening to a nationally known pastor who aligned with how I prayed and spoke boldly every week, I found myself in the book of Malachi. Full disclosure, I had not yet made it to Malachi in my two-year-long plan of reading through the Bible. Only skim-throughs of this book had given me enough information to remember Sunday school teachers talking about how the words of Malachi were the only words from God to Israel for over 400 years. I didn't know much about this book other than it was heavy with prophecy. And in that season of frustration and uncertainty of God's better plan, any bit of prophecy I could get my hands on, well, I clung to it. The chapter heading of Malachi 4 reads "The Great Day of the Lord." Well, now you've got my attention. The world needed (and still does) a great move of God. I was in!

> For behold, the day is coming, burning like an oven, when all the arrogant and all evildoers will be stubble. The day that is coming shall set them ablaze, says the Lord of hosts, so that it will leave them neither root nor branch. But for you who fear my name, the **sun of righteousness shall rise with healing in its wings**. You shall go out leaping like calves from the stall. And you shall tread down the wicked, for they will be ashes under the soles of your feet, on the day when I act, says the Lord of hosts. (Malachi 4:1-3, emphasis mine)

The sun of righteousness will rise. Wait, this reminds me of something—Jesus, the light of the world!

I recalled the second half of my friend's prophetic word: "Don't be afraid of the light." Don't be afraid of the light of holiness that disinfects impurities from dark forces of corruption, deceit, evil in the world. Don't be afraid of the light of the Son that will rise! There are so many layers to this declarative prophetic word, but I finally felt peace in drawing out the word and adding it to my prayers for our nation.

The context of this passage drives the ultimate point that those who fear the Lord should be set apart in the light of Christ's righteousness. A few verses later, Malachi then alludes to Elijah the prophet and a coming one with a ministry voice that disrupts the spirit of religion and complacency. This was, in fact, later seen in the Gospels to be lived out by John the Baptist.

Before he was even born, this John the baptizer would be called to a radical life of consecration. Luke 1 tells us an angel proclaimed to Zachariah that his son would be great before the Lord, that he would not drink wine but instead be filled with the Holy Spirit. The angel continues to amp things up with declarations that John would be called a prophet of the Most High and go before the coming Lord to prepare His way with messages of salvation and repentance. What a declaration to absorb before the boy was even born.

As John matured into his ministry, you could find him living in the wilderness, which symbolizes in the Word an intimate life with God. He was the real deal as he ate locusts and wore garments of camels' hair. He was all in on this desert life, this set-apart life interwoven and consumed with the coming Christ. Then a word from God came, breaking the centuries-long dry spell.

> The word of God came to John the son of Zechariah in the wilderness . . . The voice of one crying in the wilderness: Prepare the way of the Lord, make his paths straight. Every valley shall be filled, and every moun-

tain and hill shall be made low, and the crooked shall become straight, and the rough places shall become level ways, and all flesh shall see the salvation of God. (Luke 3:2,4-6)

Anyone in voice range to this desert call and anyone with Old Testament knowledge of the words of the prophet Isaiah would know this was a call to prepare the way for the coming king as they did in ancient days by going ahead to remove obstacles from the road and scope out straight paths for the caravan to make its way through. They would also know the symbolism in these words: the proud and the arrogant would be humbled; the humble would be lifted up. And John took things to the next level with his ministry of baptism by water and in repentance—a call to purity and holiness. This baptizer was intense in all the best ways and stirred up trouble for himself for sure. Many speculated he was the Christ, to which John was quick to proclaim he was not even worthy to tie the straps of the sandals of the coming Messiah. He was also quick to proclaim that this baptism by water in repentance would be upstaged by Jesus who would come to baptize with the Holy Spirit and with fire. Did those listening even comprehend what that meant? Probably not.

Baptism of the Holy Spirit: the blessing of the power of the Holy Spirit, the indwelling of God Himself.

Fire: purifying and also that of judgment.

The Old Testament brings us into understanding of the symbolism (and reality) of fire representing the presence of God. But this baptism of the Holy Spirit and of fire brings a burning of purity and holiness that consumes everything that is impure. Those standing out in the hot sun of John's desert would know this Old Testament context. You and I, living on this side of the cross of Christ, would know who it was who brings Spirit, power, fire of God Himself—Jesus!

Might we live as those who make ready? Those who are set apart like John and go to extremes of living all-in lifestyles of holiness declaring the kingdom of heaven and not stopping till the earth looks like heaven?

As my friend said in her prophetic word, don't be afraid of the light of glory.

Don't be afraid of the light of glory but be willing to daily be purified by the power of the Spirit.

Don't be afraid of the light of His glory and fire. This pursuit of holiness is hard and heavy but He holds your heart ever so tenderly while He strips away sin, old patterns, old wounds. There is healing in His wings, as we read in Malachi 4.

Don't be afraid of the light, and recognize darkness and corruption for what they are. My husband gave me side-eyes when I expressed some wild theories of what is behind the wild happenings in our world. And my retort to his side-eyes was the exclamation that just because we, as sinful but normal human beings, don't have the purview to even comprehend the depths of darkness, that doesn't mean it's not prevalent and active! And just because we as the Western church don't make space for the Spirit of the living God, that doesn't mean He's not alive and active. Our apathy and desire to sit on the couch of complacent faith in no way dampen the very real light and glory of God. We must rise up and contend. We must not be fooled and led astray because we choose not to see with spiritual eyes the layers of what is really moving in our world today. Eyes to see, ears to hear, and the power of the Spirit to know the Kingdom ways to push back the darkness—this is the order of the hour, Church!

Don't be afraid of the light, and take a stand. Pray like never before. Put a stake in the ground and declare that Jesus, the Son of righteousness, is Lord and is coming soon.

And in this determination to live like John, set apart in intimate relationship with the Father, to be boldly built up to declare Kingdom come, let the fire burn in you. Don't be afraid of the vulnerable and the uncomfortable moments that purify. Make ready! Tell of salvation and the Savior. Get real about sin and repentance. Love radically while you do. Worship like the undignified David in his priestly linen ephod.

Go low in humility.

Rise up to proclaim the fame of Jesus.

Make ready—swing wide the gates of your heart, city, nation that the King of glory would come in.

Grab your journal and Bible.

What extremes are you willing to go to to live set apart, to live holy? Take John the Baptist for example. His alternative lifestyle set him up to be ready to proclaim the coming of Jesus.

What do you need to say no to in order to pursue holiness?

HIGHER PURSUIT: PURSUIT OF HOLINESS

What do you need to say a holy yes to?

What comforts do you find in your life that need to be set aside? Any fears in your pursuit of holiness? Fear of letting go of those comforts? Why or why not?

DAY 3: NAME OF GOD: I AM

Moses was exiled to the desert wilderness after committing a crime. He was a man, born of Israel, raised in Egyptian courts, who saw the oppression against his people and raged against one of the oppressors. But in fleeing to the dry, hot wilderness, Moses positioned himself to not only hear from the God of Abraham but also to be commissioned by Him.

Take off your shoes, for you stand on holy ground. A normal occurrence of a burning bush was a sign of the holy, consuming fire of the great I AM. You see, the bush on fire, pure and holy, didn't burn—a sign and wonder for Moses that he received a visitation.

I see the affliction and suffering of My people. You, Moses, will be the one to set the captives free.

But who are you?

I AM who I AM.

> God said to Moses, "I am who I am." And he said, "Say this to the people of Israel: 'I am has sent me to you.'" God also said to Moses, "Say this to the people of Israel: 'The Lord, the God of your fathers, the God of Abraham, the God of Isaac, and the God of Jacob, has sent me to you.' This is my name forever, and thus I am to be remembered throughout all generations." (Exodus 3:14-16)

To declare oneself as I AM is to declare oneself as Yahweh—the sacred name to which the chosen ones call Him LORD.

All Existing One.

The One who was, is, and is to come.

The One whose very presence calls for fear, awe and wonder.

The One who offered Himself as the sacrifice for the sins of a fallen world. The One who claimed Himself I AM when the soldiers came to arrest Him and crucify Him. Upon declaring Himself I AM, they fell backward to the ground. The power of divine revelation of God Himself will do that.

> Then Jesus, knowing all that would happen to him, came forward and said to them, "Whom do you seek?" They answered him, "Jesus of Nazareth." Jesus said to them, "I am he." Judas, who betrayed him, was standing with them. When Jesus said to them, "I am he," they drew back and fell to the ground. (John 18:4-6)

The same One who commanded Moses to take off his dusty sandals for he stood on holy ground calls you and me to live in that holy space as well. The fire that miraculously did not consume the bush in the wilderness is, in fact, an all-consuming fire of purity and holiness. We don't have to question who is calling us to live in holiness or the standard by which He deems it holy. God, the One who was, is, and is to come is never-changing.

Doesn't the world offer a moving target? Yes, it does! By scrolling, swiping, liking, the standard of what is meaningful and elevated changes at the whim of even those deemed as "Christian influencers." And how often do we fall for and fall short of this moving target in the effort to grab hold of worth and meaning in life?

To pursue holiness and worship the great I AM is to long for that which offers eternal stability, because you know the promise of the great shaking:

> At that time his voice shook the earth, but now he has promised, "Yet once more I will shake not only the earth but also the heavens." This phrase, "Yet once more," indicates the removal of things that are shaken—that is, things that have been made—in order that the things that cannot be shaken may remain. Therefore let us be grateful for receiving a kingdom that cannot be shaken, and thus let us offer to God acceptable worship, with reverence and awe, for our God is a consuming fire. (Hebrews 12:26-29)

Yes, He is the all-consuming fire. An unshakable Savior. The One and Only who never changes no matter the whims of humans. He also promises that the best will be left behind in His shaking—heavenly things, Kingdom things, eternal things that reflect His glory and beauty. I don't know about you, but I would rather start now grasping tightly to those unshakeable facets rather than chase the wind and waste time.

So this begs the question: In your higher pursuits, after coming before the Lord with awe and wonder, after holding His presence like gold, in your daily pursuit of holiness, what will you align with? Who will you align with? Will it be the moving target that seems easy, fun, without any sacrifice?

Will you align with corruption and the very real and present darkness by sticking your head in the sand, thus denying the need to be the very salt that preserves from corruption and the light that purifies darkness?

Will you stay silent and willfully ignorant?

Or will you decide to be holy because He calls you to be holy to usher purity and righteousness into your every square inch?

The pursuit of holiness is the pursuit of God Himself—not for the sake of earning heaven when you die, or for checking the box as a "good Christian girl." To pursue holiness is to align your whole life with I AM as an act of worship and desire to live out "kingdom come," as Jesus taught the disciples to pray. It's an act of covering yourself in the righteousness of Christ, for He brought you back to right standing, full communion, with the All Existing One. Yes, this is a higher pursuit worth the sacrifice that comes with denying yourself. Because the unshakeable reward of life abundant is worth it. He, the I AM, is worthy of it all.

We will get gritty with this in the next two sections. But in this moment, let's swim in the knowledge of the glory (*fire!*) of the Lord, in the face of Christ Jesus, by the power of the Holy Spirit.

Grab your journal and Bible.

Let's return to the discipline of simply writing out the Word to allow it to soak into our spirit and soul. Grab your journal and write out some or all of these suggested scriptures:

>I AM verses of Jesus:
>I am the Bread of Life. (John 6:35)
>I am the Light of the World. (John 8:12)
>I am the Door. (John 10:9)
>I am the Good Shepherd. (John 10:11,14)
>I am the Resurrection and the Life. (John 11:25)
>I am the Way and the Truth and the Life. (John 14:6)

I am the Vine. (John 15:1,5)

Be still and know that I AM God. (Psalm 46:10)

Read Revelation 22 and write out any verses that the Holy Spirit highlights.

What in your life is shakeable that you cling tightly to? What in your life is Kingdom strong and unshakeable?

Describe in your own words I AM, the all-consuming fire of purity and holiness.

DAY 4: SPIRITUAL DISCIPLINE: WORSHIP

There is this wild, awesome church in Arizona that has been living in sustained revival for the last seven years (at the time I write this book). Fresh Start Revival Church operates in a lifestyle of worship. They call it High Praise. Each time the congregation meets, a group preps the room with pre-service prayer as the drums keep a warfare beat in the background. Then, with so much intentionality and purpose, the church moves into exuberant, loud, uncorrupted worship to push back the enemy and call down heaven. Singing in tongues is part of their culture. No one bats an eye. And there was that time when the worship leaders literally fell to their knees under the weight of God's glory that fell over the room. They groaned and sang into the mic out of pure, raw worship of the King of glory. It is a wild dynamic for sure. I love it!

I also very much honor and respect worship environments that are more somber and subdued yet filled with the presence of God. Jesus told the woman at the well that the Father is looking for worshipers who worship Him in spirit and in truth (see John 4:23-24). This can happen in wild and loud rooms of raw singing and in more subdued situations as long as the intensity of passion is there.

Regardless of the manner in which we worship, the Holy Spirit helps us to see God rightly. To see Him rightly is to worship the full truth of who God is. We are not called to cherry-pick and worship only the parts of God that make us feel good at any given moment.

Worship is a spiritual discipline because it takes cutting away our self-focused, "it's all about me" posture and turning our entire being to the Higher Pursuit of looking at God at one angle and then crying, "HOLY, HOLY, HOLY!"—and then turning our head a bit, seeing the throne of grace at a different angle, and crying, "HOLY, HOLY, HOLY!"

Now, get out of your seat, walk over to the other side of the room filled with the train of His robe (see Isaiah 6), and cry, "HOLY, HOLY, HOLY! LORD! Show me more of who You are!"

Worship isn't only defined as standing in a room with a band playing and words on a screen. Worship can be something like flipping through this book to grab a name of God as you sit and write out your own psalm of thanksgiving and praise. The Higher Pursuit here is a lifestyle of worship—a holistic lifestyle. Remember that our "every square inch" goes for worship too!

For me, the discipline of prayer and worship when I am alone is something to constantly build. My attention span is embarrassingly short and though I am worshiping the One who is worthy, it's my phone that is so easily accessible to hold in my hand and feel it's presence and weight right in front of me. It takes grit and holy desperation to push away the temptation to pick it up. And on those days when I'm just not feeling it and hit a wall, the phone is there to entertain me.

Maybe you do the same?

Let's commit to building the discipline of undistracted worship.

First, if the distractions creep in, commit to immediately dismissing them in your mind. I like to imagine that the distraction is a box floating by on a conveyor belt. I take the box and imagine that I'm placing it on a table beside me. I "table" it for later, as they say in the business world. This actually goes for prayer too.

Second, move your body. You don't have to be the one who waves her arms all round, but there is something to be said for moving and engaging with the song.

Third, kneel. This is a similar concept but with the motivation of surrender. The physical act of surrender moves mountains in my spirit as I worship.

Finally, default to worship. We as Kingdom women, with the resources of heaven, should never be bored. Waiting in line? Sing a song. Folding laundry? Tell Him who He is. Meal prepping for the week? Praise! Empty moments in our day are divine opportunities to tap into those hidden places of heaven as we join in with the angels: "HOLY, HOLY, HOLY!"

Notice how I didn't once say anything about how you will feel because of worship. Our Higher Pursuit offers the goal only to pour out. Refreshment will come because God is that good. Worship is a calling not for your own pursuit of purpose or to feel good but simply because *He is worthy*. Period.

Grab your journal and your Bible.

Simply grab your Bible and sit with a couple of these suggested scriptures. To build your muscles of the discipline of worship, commit yourself to a segment of time that stretches your normal attention span. Write out these verses. Write out praises. Write out fears and worries in light of who God is in His Word. Praise God for who He is. This is your act of worship for today. Do it again tomorrow for a little longer. And then the next day, a little longer. The desire will grow day by day when you just show up with a soft heart.

Suggested scriptures: Psalm 145; Psalm 139; Colossians 1; Philippians 2:5-11

DAY 5: EVERYDAY REVIVAL-DECISION POINT

Let's touch base again on revival: what is it? Revival is not just a feeling or a "zing" of the Holy Spirit. Revival is an awakening of the heart, soul, mind, and strength to the power and glory of God. And at the same time that there is an arising and awakening, there is an all-out surrender before the cross of Christ. A body in motion of praise is also laid out in surrender because they've come to the end of self and nothing else will sustain but the all-consuming power, love, mercy, kindness of God. Do you see that holy paradox: arise/awake, go low in surrender?

We've seen glorious corporate and regional moves of God in history when the Spirit of the living God poured out and people were radically transformed—cities were radically shifted under the fear of God Himself. As I read revival history accounts, I long to see that for myself. In fact, over the past year, I've traveled on my own revival adventures to go where God is moving. It's said in history that people would travel to the revival region, catch the spark in repentance and worship, and then literally bring back the spark for revival to break out in their own area. Like sparks of wildfires, the Holy Spirit moved and brought people into repentance and salvation with the weight of glory poured out over a city or town. My own revival adventures sparked a longing for the fire. I'm a "go big or go home" kind of person, and over the past year, I've been on my knees for that bonfire of the Holy Spirit to light up in my own region with wild worship of Jesus, signs and wonders, and droves of people surrendering their life to the Lord.

And while I diligently pray and gather other prayer warriors and worshipers, the Lord has shown me that lighting the fire of the desire for holiness and purity out of fear of God sparks an everyday kind of revival.

Ephesians 5:18 tells us to refrain from drunkenness that dulls the fire of holiness, but instead be filled—continually filled—with the Holy Spirit. We will dive into the pursuit of the Spirit in an upcoming chapter, but might we camp out with the revival call to every day be filled continually? Open up that tap of flowing power already poured out on Pentecost! We don't have to beg for it, for it was already poured out in great measure 2,000 years ago. The floodgates were opened. Will we choose daily to tap into the power, wisdom, presence of God Himself? This is surrender: to acknowledge a mightier force than our own will, desires, agenda; to say, "Let it be so, Lord! Revive my heart in the flow of the Spirit. Cleanse my hands. Move and live in me. Not my will but *Yours* be done." This is everyday revival. It's a decision point. It's a place of alignment. The pursuit of holiness positions us to align our thoughts, words, actions, heart posture with that which pleases the good Father—with that which is actually good by design.

I find it so interesting that Paul encourages the Ephesians to be continually filled by the Spirit right after a strong exhortation to awake from slumber, to pursue godliness, to walk in the light, and to expose darkness.

> . . . for at one time you were darkness, but now you are light in the Lord. Walk as children of light (for the fruit of light is found in all that is good and right and true), and try to discern what is pleasing to the Lord. Take no part in the unfruitful works of darkness, but instead expose them. (Ephesians 5:8-11)

"What is pleasing to the Lord"—this is the pursuit of holiness out of devotion, out of awe and wonder, out of the desire for closeness as you seek His face.

The Voice translation says to "make it your aim to learn what pleases the

Lord." That seems like the onus is on you and me to journey through life with soft hearts and a desire to look around every corner of our day to find what is holy, pure, and righteous, and then to partner with that in thought, word, and deed.

To ask this question daily—"What pleases You, Lord?"—is not to perform for revival but to make ready for a move of God in you and through you as you walk as a child of the light, as Paul proclaims. The fruit of light found in all that is good, right, and true reflects to the world around you, your every square inch, the beauty and goodness that God originally intended for creation. A pursuit of holiness is a partnership with the Kingdom not out of obligation but out of the knowledge that it's a privilege to daily live in revival by the power of the Holy Spirit.

To ask this question daily—"What pleases You, Lord?"—is the sacred act of tending to the fires of the altar of His presence. Romans 12:1 tells us that our life is a living sacrifice; it is not our own.

> I appeal to you therefore, brothers, by the mercies of God, to present your bodies as a living sacrifice, holy and acceptable to God, which is your spiritual worship. Do not be conformed to this world, but be transformed by the renewal of your mind, that by testing you may discern **what is the will of God, what is good and acceptable and perfect**. (Romans 12:1, emphasis mine)

The Higher Pursuit of holiness positions us to live as light and salt that preserve purity and fend off corruption. Tending to the fires of the altar of His presence in our life is like building a fire with wood and kindling. Dry, ready wood best sparks a fire full of warmth and power. Keeping our altar ready comes with that constant act of confession and repentance. And the Higher Pursuit, to take it further, is the moment-by-moment decision to say yes to holiness because it's not just a list of "thou shall nots." It's a divine privilege to partner with a yes to holiness, not for winning God's love or approval, but to shower Him with honor and reverence in our holy choices every day.

Grab your Journal.

Grab your Bible and read Titus 2:11-14 as you write out a phrase or two from this passage to stay engaged with the scripture. Honing in on verses 11-12, how are we able to train ourselves for godliness? What is it about the grace of God that stirs you toward a pursuit of holiness?

Do a brain dump: take an honest look, at the ungodliness in your life. What do you watch that does not please God? What do you say? Do? Think? This is not for condemnation, but just to get real and raw.

Let's not stop there though. In order to be continually filled with the Spirit and to keep the altar burning for God's presence, remind yourself what fruits of the Spirit the Lord has graced you with. Read Galatians 5:22-24 and write out each fruit to say yes to in pursuing holiness.

What fruit can you lean into today as your yes to holiness, as your act of worship? Write out a prayer of declaration.

CHAPTER 5

HIGHER PURSUIT: HOLY DESPERATION

DAY 1: FLIP THE SCRIPT

I wonder if today would be a good day to flip the script. Hard, heavy, sharp edges around us might lead us to desperation, to hopelessness. Do we have to drown in it? No way! Add the word "holy" to the word "desperation" and that's how we change the world around us—that's how we create space for Jesus to change things.

Holy desperation leads to revival. It calls forth deep hunger and realization that the end of our self (pride, ego, anger, jealousy, comparison—whatever is your sin of choice at any given moment) brings us to a decision point: to hunger and hold our hands open to God's fullness *or* to keep with the status quo of hopelessness.

A holy desperation for God Himself to move—yes, this is what brings revival.

Because of the cross, we don't have to operate in death but in life filled with forgiveness, justice, mercy, *love*. Because He rose from the grave, because He is coming again, because He sent His Holy Spirit to comfort and bring us power (wrapped in perfect love), a holy desperation is called for. God's *more* is the driving force of our hope-filled desperation—not the perceived abundance or even the very real depravity of our world around us.

But we must come to the end of our self and yearn for the One who is our perfect reconciliation to God's original design for His creation: perfect unity with the Father. This brings peace, joy, love. Might I say peace again? Shalom!

A holy desperation for God Himself is our first and only option, not our last resort.

Desperate because we know that God's presence changes everything. Thank You, Jesus, for the cross.

I just need you to hear this today: The world *will* continue spin out and get darker and darker. But God's glory and power will shine brighter and brighter.

What will you align with?

Will you align with the Kingdom and actively push back darkness? Or will you cower in fear, listening to and heeding the narratives of those who are actively deceiving the masses—those who are partnering with the enemy of your soul? There's a real tension there.

It's the call of John the Baptist: Make ready for the King of Glory.

John the Baptist was a wild man who moved in the wilderness rather than in the norms of the society of his day, a wild radical calling out the need for repentance, a man who knew that the One whose sandals he was not even worthy to carry was coming to shake the kingdom of the world to its core.

> I ritually cleanse you through baptism as a mark of turning your life around. But someone is coming after me, someone whose sandals I am not fit to carry, someone who is more powerful than I. He will wash you not in water but in fire and with the Holy Spirit. (Matthew 3:11, The Voice)

To make ready—to prepare the way—is to position ourselves in holy desperation for Jesus, who is our only option. It's through worship with awe and wonder. It's through moment-by-moment repentance, because new mercies come every moment. It's through bold declarations with words and actions that show the world who is coming and who is worthy.

It's the cry of Elijah to push back against the evil embedded in high places of government and even in the Church.

Elijah was a prophet who heard the voice of God Himself and pushed back on the corrupt king and queen duo: Ahab and Jezebel. In his holy desperation, fueled by the knowledge of the power of the living God, he stood alone and called down idol worship in Israel. Lighting an impossible fire because the altar was soaked in water, the living God (not Baal!) called His nation back to repentance and to His presence. This is all because of one brave man who knew the depths of evil and also that abundance of light, glory, power in the one true God.

> And when all the people saw it, they fell on their faces and said, "The Lord, he is God; the Lord, he is God." (1 Kings 18:39)

It's not time to play. These lesser pursuits that Christians have been playing around with in the meantime aren't going to cut it. Some of these lesser pursuits have looked like things such as, fear of man or being politically correct. Other lesser pursuits that won't keep us steadfast is the obsession with pursuing goals and dreams while the world around us is going haywire. I also see too many women getting caught up in the gloss of social media when people must see real, raw, and authentic Christians concerned with things of God rather than building their platform. Instead, we are called to make ready and operate in Higher Pursuits of the fear of God, discerning the times (open your eyes!), seeking His face, and filled with the power of Holy Spirit.

If you've cowered in fear and succumbed to the narrative, it's not too late. Repent, align with the light and with awe and wonder of the only One who can save us. Actively push back. Pray. Fast. Speak out. Love. Offer mercy.

A move of God is the only answer right now. Make ready!

Grab your Bible and journal.

We have come this far in our Higher Pursuits to understand the priority of seeking God's face; to live with awe, wonder, reverence; to pursue holiness; to hold the Word in value. Do you see the need, now, to flip the script? How does holy desperation play into this life of Higher Pursuits?

Grab your Bible and a Bible app to read a couple different translations of Psalm 84. Read slowly and intentionally. Go ahead and write out several of the verses to further interact with scripture.

HIGHER PURSUIT: HOLY DESPERATION

> How lovely is your dwelling place, O Lord of hosts! My soul longs, yes, faints for the courts of the Lord; my heart and flesh sing for joy to the living God. Even the sparrow finds a home, and the swallow a nest for herself, where she may lay her young, at your altars, O Lord of hosts, my King and my God. Blessed are those who dwell in your house, ever singing your praise! Selah. (Psalm 84:1-2)

This might not yet be your level of desperation, and that's okay! Wherever you are, we will dive deeper together and go from glory to glory in our understanding. Might I offer you some prayer points to stir your soul? Finish off these prayer starters in your journal.

> Lord, show me where anything but Your presence falls way short...
> Thank You, Jesus, for the cross that made the way for me to enter the courts of Your presence...
> Stir up my holy desperation for You and for Your kingdom to advance...
> Amen!

DAY 2: "BLESSED ARE THOSE..."—BEATITUDES AND HOLY DESPERATION

Since we are on the topic of flipping the script, it's important to also redirect our personal narrative surrounding happiness and the pursuit of happiness. Did you know that Jesus had twelve verses worth to say about happiness? He did! And what Jesus said about even the pursuit of happiness counters our own narrative and that of the culture around us, which elevates success, achievement, climbing the ladder toward the illusion of what will offer joy and contentment—happiness as the world defines it.

I'm wondering if you are scratching your head, recalling the Gospels, and asking where Jesus in fact mentions happiness. I would be as well. You see, in Matthew 5, Jesus begins His Sermon on the Mount with what is commonly known as the Beatitudes. That word "Beatitude" means "the blessings." And, thus, we find ourselves in a conversation about happiness. But this is not one you will find in self-help books or even books cloaked with scripture that point you to live your #bestlife. These Beatitudes point to the blessing that comes with developing the character of someone who has a holy desperation to be a kingdom citizen. In twelve verses, Jesus offers blessings that offer happiness. Let me explain.

The word "blessing" in the original Greek has a connotation for our topic at hand: happiness. But we must not read that through the lens of Western culture or even Western Christianity. In the original understanding of the word Jesus used for blessing, He was pointing to an ultimate satisfaction, joy, and yes, happiness found when living out the words that followed each "Blessed are you . . ." For in this word "blessed," there is also found a connotation of joy/happiness that doesn't waver depending on life's circumstances. This is further enriched by the kingdom characteristics spelled out in each Beatitude.

Something has happened through the filtering of the Word in a modern/

Western mindset. The Beatitudes have been misused (as has much of the Bible) to support things like earthly and temporary suffering. And while I know that the Word of God is active and alive to comfort those who are poor, who suffer, who mourn loss, this particular passage in the Bible is really only about a spiritual framework to be a citizen of heaven—not a citizen of this very broken world.

This is such good news. Why? Because, when we live out these Beatitudes, we are set up to weather the very real storms life brings with suffering and loss. The foundation is the character that is asked of us as followers of Christ, and we find happiness, joy, and blessing when posturing ourselves in what is described in the Beatitudes. I think you will be delighted to tie in your Higher Pursuit of holy desperation as you read these words from Jesus.

But first, a list. I love a good list, don't you?

- Poor in spirit
- Mourn
- Meek
- Hunger and thirst
- Merciful
- Peacemakers
- Persecuted
- Reviled

Take in those words. Read that list a couple of times. Those words don't scream out to you a recipe for happiness and success, do they? Nope. Not under an earthly, temporal filter. But, under the Kingdom's everlasting filter of reality, Jesus proclaims blessing and happiness when living out this very list.

> Blessed are the **poor in spirit**, for theirs is the kingdom of heaven. (Matthew 5:3, emphasis mine)

The question for us then is, what defines poor in spirit when we usually only talk about poverty in a monetary sense? I think we already know the answer as women who live in the Higher Pursuit of fear of God and who live in a posture of confession and repentance. It's more than an acknowledgment of our sin; it's the knowledge of the reality that we have nothing, no spiritual equity or assets (poor), without the grace and mercy of God in the knowledge of Christ's redemption at the cross. My goodness, if I want to live in the abundant reality of the Kingdom of heaven, not even a hint of an attitude of being "holier than thou" can slip from my thoughts and words toward others. So, might we just be so very grateful the Lord gives us the Holy Spirit as a seal on our life to lead us to recognize our poverty of spirit because we have the knowledge of the glory of God?!

Charles Spurgeon makes such a beautiful point: "Everyone can start here; it isn't first blessed are the pure or the holy or the spiritual or the wonderful. Everyone can be poor in spirit. 'Not what I have, but what I have not,' is the first point of contact, between my soul and God."

I have not glory in me, elevation, renown, fame, pride, when I behold the infinite value of the glory of God. My soul is separated from everything that makes me whole without God's love and mercy shown in the face of Christ Jesus. And happiness, contentment, satisfaction come into play when we actively weigh out what we leave behind (earthly assets and gain) and what we *get to behold* in eternity. There's no way to truly grasp it this side of heaven, but that is the blessedness found in a life of holy desperation. Nothing will satisfy, so I will surrender to the glory of God, live with a desperation for holiness and heaven, and seek "Kingdom come" while my feet walk the earth for as long as God calls me to it.

Humility positions us for the blessing of beholding the glory of God.

> "Blessed are **those who mourn**, for they shall be comforted" (Matthew 5:4, emphasis added).

It's important to note here that though Jesus comforts those who mourn in loss and suffering, this verse has a different context for mourning. The original language uses several levels of intensity of mourning, and this verse uses the strongest form. What Jesus is digging into is the deep grief over the fallen state and the sin of the world. It is also applied individually to our own sin as we grieve what actions, words, thoughts displease God. So, what blessing actually comes from mourning? That we don't have to stay in mourning and grief but can move to thanksgiving and joy because we are forgiven and set free of the bondage of sin. The posture of holy desperation is not about ultimate despair. Remember the word "holy" in front of it. We are desperately aware of the righteousness, power, purity, love, mercy of God in the face of real depravity of sin and its effects on our world.

It is a desperation for what is to come: that Jesus returns in victory over the evil and darkness. We will touch on this in the next section, but in the meantime, I invite you to meditate on what joy comes from the knowledge of the glory and victory of God over that which grieves you.

> "Blessed are the **meek**, for they shall inherit the earth" (Matthew 5:5, emphasis added).

I've wrestled with that word, meek, before I understood what Jesus meant in this passage. Meek is not weakness or to be quiet and unseen. Simply put, biblical meekness is actually a strength under submission to God through the leading of Holy Spirit. Take this for example. Meekness is like a being a well trained horse that is full of power well under control. A well trained horse is ready to race toward the purposes of the Kingdom. Imagine if Christians lived fully ourselves with talents and resources completely trained for and eyes set on the work of the kingdom. We would be free and powerful to give all for Him. And in this strength under submission to God and His word, we find ourselves living in humility, in service to others, with patience, gentleness and more. This is all to the ultimate reward and blessing of inheritance.

With holy desperation, we look to the blessing bestowed when God allows us to live on Earth in His fullness as we steward His grace and goodness for others to behold His beauty within creation all around.

> "Blessed are those who **hunger and thirst for righteousness**, for they shall be satisfied" (Matthew 5:6, emphasis added).

I think that you and I have come to this Beatitude with some great foundational understanding of hunger and thirst for righteousness, especially after we have explored the Higher Pursuit of the fear of God and the pursuit of holiness. But we can always be reminded of the banqueting table overflowing with satisfying, rich fruit of our pursuits because we truly hunger and long for the righteousness of God to prevail in every square inch of the world. Know that this pursuit is not in vain. Joy and happiness come in the satisfying knowledge that the glory of God (His righteousness and wrath, love and mercy) will prevail, as we read in Habakkuk 2:14. We would do well to keep this in mind as we pray and intercede for our city, nation, and the world to bubble up in a glorious harvest of souls surrendering to Jesus as King and Lord. The day is coming. Don't despair without hope in the meantime. Live in a holy desperation that He is on the move. While you are at it, enjoy the rich food at the table of satisfying abundance to which you are invited because of your holy desperation for righteousness.

> "Blessed are the **merciful**, for they shall receive mercy. Blessed are the **pure in heart**, for they shall see God. Blessed are the **peacemakers**, for they shall be called sons of God" (Matthew 5:7 emphasis added).

Isn't it so kind of God to give us a humble, kind place to land after that strong Beatitude regarding righteousness? We find happiness and joy when seeking the sharp (and good) edges that can be found in righteousness, and we find happiness when we pair that sharp edge with mercy, a pure heart, and life as a peacemaker. To go after the sharp edge and then the softer side is to find mercy for ourselves because we need forgiveness and grace too, lest we forget. We have the privilege of seeking God Himself because of our pure heart devoid of pride, sin, self-focus. And we get to go after peace that is shalom and not just peace for the sake of no violence and strife, though that is a worthy pursuit as well. In these words of Jesus, He is going after a messianic peace, which is encompassed in the Jewish word *shalom*. The meaning of shalom is complex; but in not-so-simple words, it means well-being and in the fullness of Christ. We can recall our biblical worldview term "reconciliation" and apply it to being a peacemaker who is blessed and happy. To seek what Christ seeks: that the whole earth be brought back to the original intent of a loving Father, and that His created ones be cleansed of sin and brought back into His holy presence—that is a peacemaker's goal. To seek the welfare of their city, nation, world in light of God's love for His creation. You can't do this without a pure heart for God, which leads to a posture of mercy. I just love how God's Word is synergistic and works together.

> "Blessed are those who are **persecuted for righteousness'** sake, for theirs is the kingdom of heaven. Blessed are you when others **revile you and persecute you** and utter all kinds of evil against you **falsely on my account**. Rejoice and be glad, for your reward is great in heaven, for so they persecuted the prophets who were before you." (Matthew 5:10-12, emphasis added).

A life filled with Higher Pursuits, such as the fear of God, to seek His face, to go after holiness, and be filled with the Spirit, is a life acutely aware of the coming days when even those in the West who are used to a cushy, Christian life will be persecuted. Jesus is so kind in His offering of blessing and happiness to those of us in the future and to those who listened to Him at the time of His earthly ministry. Many of them did, in fact, face horrific persecution after the Church was filled with the fire of God and sent out to the ends of the earth to tell of the good news. To be aware of even modern-day persecution is to understand the times we are in.

Awareness. Readiness. Standing firm. Being bold with humility and meekness. Knowing the Word. Knowing the knowledge of the glory of God. Equipped in the day that is to come. These are all elements of the Higher Pursuits put to action.

And in the depths of darkness of persecution, there is great joy in the unexplainable glory and light of God. It will get darker. But His glory will shine brighter and revival will come. Many are seeing revival already. This is the joy and delight awaiting those in Higher Pursuit.

Grab your Bible and journal.

Reread the Beatitudes (Matthew 5:3-12) and write down the list from above that states the 8 characteristics of those who are blessed. Add in some bullet points to sum up each "Blessed are..." statement.

We can look at each of the Beatitudes as heart postures and even lifestyle choices. Get real and nitty-gritty here; which heart posture is hardest for you to take? Why? Which one comes more naturally?

Write out what it means to be "blessed" in the context of Jesus' words in the Beatitudes. Do you see how this heart posture, lifestyle choice, thought process differs from the hustle culture and self-focused nature of our world? How does this reframe your desire to operate in holy desperation as a Higher Pursuit?

Take time in your journal to pray through this list of Beatitudes as your higher pursuit today.

DAY 3: NAME OF GOD: THE LION AND THE LAMB

Just as Mary poured out her expensive oil at the feet of Jesus, did you know those same oils and spices are used to prepare the dead for burial? Isn't it interesting that Mary chose to break a bottle also used for such a specific purpose? I believe it was quite intentional. This is total speculation, of course, as it doesn't say this in the Bible, but I have to believe that this woman, who spent day in and day out listening to the teachings of Jesus, would especially pay attention to the words He spoke regarding His impending death and resurrection. I mean, hello! Those are big topics and ground to cover while walking the hillsides of Israel, right? Yet, the other disciples missed it. Denied it. Ran in fear when they came after Jesus.

But Mary.

She heard.

She listened.

She made ready.

And with holy desperation, even without fully understanding, she acted in faith and poured out her life's savings in that expensive bottle on Jesus in recognition and in worship that He is the Lamb who would be slain.

I think of you and me in this pursuit of holy desperation. Do we lean on every single word He says? We live on this side of the cross of Christ, in a place where most of us have so much access to resources to build our faith and knowledge of the things of God. How many Bibles do you have at home? I have a whole stack of them! Do we lean in and really listen? Do we listen and then make ready like Mary?

Lion and the Lamb

Yes, we worship Him as the perfect and holy sacrifice for our sins—the Lamb who was slain. But to make ready in these wild days we live in, we must look to the Lion of Judah as well. The Lion who is coming with a mighty roar to bring judgment.

> And one of the elders said to me, "Weep no more; behold, the Lion of the tribe of Judah, the Root of David, has conquered, so that he can open the scroll and its seven seals." (Revelation 5:5)

Though we won't dive into eschatology (end-times theology) in this space, we will recognize that Jesus is coming back as the victorious Lion with a mighty roar.

> I looked up and saw that heaven had opened. Suddenly, a white horse appeared. Its rider is called Faithful and True, and with righteousness He exercises judgment and wages war. His eyes burn like a flaming fire, and on His head are many crowns. His name was written before the creation of the world, and no one knew it except He Himself. He is dressed in a robe dipped in blood, and the name He was known by is The Word of God. (Revelation 19:11-13, The Voice)

There were twelve tribes in ancient Israel, one of them being Judah. What's special about this tribe is that it was known as the "kingly tribe" and that King David was born out of this special group of Israelites. We also know that Jesus was the eternal fulfillment of the role of King and that He was born out of the lineage of David, thus Judah. There are multiple references of lions in the Old Testament and it would be good to be reminded that lions are fierce and represent majesty and power. Jesus is the ultimate fulfillment of these references to victorious lions in Scripture. And He will come and ultimately fulfill the prophecies that Satan will be conquered and that Jesus will reign forever.

I intentionally started our Higher Pursuit journey with spiritual practices and worship cues to lead us into confession and repentance as we remembered and surrendered at the cross of Christ, the Lamb who was slain. And holding that with value like gold, let's shift and consider what a life looks like that's full of expectation of the coming Lion of Judah.

"Stop lamenting for what is not and contend for what should be."

This is what I heard from the Lord after spinning myself into a tight ball of frustration and sadness over the apathy of the Church at large with the surrender to the spirit of fear and of religion. More specifically, I heard Him say that revival would not come until churches, ministries, His *people*, stop doing the business of ministry and stop trying to get back to business as usual.

But for many, many months after the world was turned upside down, this is exactly what we are still doing. This word charged me forward, and instead of grieving and lamenting for what is not, I decided to contend for what could be—what should be.

People humble before the living God. People hungry and thirsty for His presence and fullness. People set apart, not conformed to these wild anti-God mandates of the world. People not afraid to look radically different and then filled with love, who move in this world with Kingdom goodness toward reformation and transformation. This is what the eyes of God are roaming across the world looking for. The Lion of Judah is coming with a roar. Will He find these types of followers? I hope so!

A holy desperation. That is the driving force. Surrendered to the Lamb and desperate for Him to come back as the Lion.

As I've stopped lamenting and decided to contend, I've actively come before Jesus to seek His face—to know Him and be known. I've spent hours in prayers of confession and repentance, asking Him as Moses did, "Show me Your glory!" It's so very good when we rise up off the couch of complacent faith to daily worship and contend and not hold back and lament—or worse, succumb to the fear and intimidation of the devil. I decided my higher pursuit was to refuse to go back to business as usual. Too much is at stake and too much of God's presence, power, healing, mercy, forgiveness, love is available to stay where we were when things were just comfy and cozy.

This is what I've decided to declare, and I invite you into this space as well. I decided that it was time to jump in that river of living water that Jesus talks about in John 7—revival water. I'm thirsty for it. I'm desperate to the point of the end of myself where the filling of the Holy Spirit is my greatest delight. Revival isn't a catchphrase for me. I'm done lamenting for what is not. I'm on my knees contending for what should be.

The Lion of Judah is who is coming and whom I will make ready for.

Grab your Bible and journal.

As I mentioned before, while we won't get into end-times eschatology, we are after the notion of making ready for the Lion who is coming again in victory. Take a moment to assess anything you know or think you know about the end times. Any fears? Any questions? Any excitement? Go ahead and submit those to the Lord.

HIGHER PURSUITS

At the end of this chapter, we will talk about your everyday revival in the pursuit of holy desperation. We will chat about the nitty-gritty of making ready for Jesus. But let's go ahead and stir the pot by reminding ourselves *who* it is who is coming back in victory. Grab your Bible and read Revelation 19:11-13. I used The Voice translation earlier, but it would be good to add in another translation.

What does this description of Jesus stir in you? Compare and contrast it to other scriptures describing Jesus as the Lamb who was slain. Remember, He is both/and, not either/or. Hash this out in your journal.

Write a prayer asking the Lord to reveal to you ways that you may begin to make ready.

DAY 4: SPIRITUAL DISCIPLINE: FASTING

Promise me that you won't read the section title and skip it. Promise?

I'm writing this with shaky hands because I happen to be partaking in a 24-hour fast today. Let me tell you though,: I fought this whole fasting discipline for a long time. I did valid, but still less intense, fasts from television, social media, sugar—plenty of those. But to set aside food for 24 hours seemed daunting and scary. And the Lord still spoke to me through the years, even when passionate fasting was something I shied away from.

I worked up to the whole 24 hours though. A desperation for a move of God propelled me to a daily fast of not eating during the lunch hour. And let me tell you, that quickly turned into a "Daniel" fast during the lunch hours, to which I only ate nuts and fruit because I turned into Mean Mom come dinner and homework hour without a bit of food. Still, the Lord was so kind as I took that baby step. I found *closeness to the heart of my Father* when I surrendered my flesh and desire to eat my favorite Neapolitan pizza that every now and then serves as my treat lunch meal. That was motivation enough to skip lunch for weeks and be rewarded with richer worship and revelation of the nature of the Lord. I wanted more and more!

It was only until I signed up for a health and fitness program that I found myself in a 24-hour fast from food. The Lord is so kind. He used my interest in eating clean and in kick-butt workouts to move me into courage to abstain from eating for all those hours. It was through health coaching that I learned how to set myself up for a long fast and, though the program didn't include prayer and worship in the health fast, I sure did. Again, the deepened surrender of my flesh and the longing down in my belly for sustenance were met with a filling that can only ever be found in God's overwhelming presence. Each hunger pang reminded me to surrender deeper. Deep cries out to deep when you get in up to your ankles and then up to your knees and then up to your shoulders and then you might as well go all in because it's that good. He called me deeper and used the bodily (earthly/fleshly) health benefits of fasting to engage me in this fast. I just love how synergistic the Lord is.

But hear me say, *any kind of fast and surrender of fleshly desires is valid and fruitful* when done with a passion to seek His face *without* distraction.

On the other side of the act of denying your flesh is the beautiful abundance of God's presence. No, fasting isn't the only way to seek His face, to find clarity, to hear His voice. But think of fasting as a clearing away of the junk.

My garage is currently full of stuff. Much of it is good stuff that we simply need to store away appropriately. But much of what clutters that space is unnecessary and even, well, junk. When I get out of my car after a long day, all I want is a clear path to the sanctuary that is my house. Yes, I can maneuver around the junk somewhat easily, but isn't it more peaceful to walk straight in?

When I operate in holy desperation, my heart's desire is to go straight to the source. My soul longs to go straight to the One I know will cover me in peace, mercy, wisdom, clarity—Himself. For example, I'm a big-picture kind of gal and I see the global moving parts and pieces that seem to add up to a global move of evil. You don't have to see the big picture to know that Satan is ramping up his last push because he knows Jesus is coming back. Too often, though, I move into fleshly despair as I wring my hands. I collect worry and fear as clutter in my heart, mind, and soul.

But when I flip the script, holy desperation simply takes me straight into confidence that God knows, sees, and is moving. Holy desperation helps me posture myself in Spirit-led prayer out of the knowledge that God moves upon the prayers of His people. Fasting is what strips away my excess pride, sin, unrighteousness, and positions me into a deeper surrender—into His power and mercy that I so very much need.

In Matthew 17, Jesus talks about the importance of fasting: The disciples tried with all their might and prayed diligently for the child afflicted by a demon. I don't blame the desperate father for then going straight to Jesus (the Source!), who then healed the child by casting out said demon. But Jesus didn't stop there; He used this moment as a teaching point for the disciples. Might we be instructed as well?

> Because you have so little faith. I tell you this: if you had even a faint spark of faith, even faith as tiny as a mustard seed, you could say to this mountain, "Move from here to there," and because of your faith, the mountain would move. If you had just a sliver of faith, you would find nothing impossible. But this kind is not realized except through much prayer and fasting. (Matthew 17:19-21, The Voice)

Charles Spurgeon does an exquisite job summing up this passage specifically in regards to prayer and fasting: "He that would overcome the devil in certain instances must first overcome heaven by prayer, and conquer himself by self-denial."

Fasting clears the clutter. Fasting calls us into self-denial. Fasting enriches our prayer and dependence. Prayer and dependence on the

Father grow our faith. Faith drives us to move mountains in the name of Jesus. Moving mountains in the name of Jesus shows the world His power, might, love.

See how that works? I don't know about you, but that pumps me up for some more fasting!

Let's trade temporary hunger only satisfied with that which fades for holy desperation—a hunger and thirst surrendered to the only One who delights and calls us to taste and see that the Lord is good. To fast is to sit at the abundant heavenly banqueting table. Go ahead! Find your seat too.

Grab your Bible and journal.

What fears do you have about fasting?

What one area of your life is cluttered to the point that you need a fresh word from the Lord?

What confession and repentance can you bring to Him by way of focusing in and fasting?

HIGHER PURSUIT: HOLY DESPERATION

Since we are all about Higher Pursuits, ask the Lord to give you boldness to push your self-denial a bit further with regards to fasting. Can you fast lunch for a week? What about completely cutting out something that brings great pleasure to find utmost delight in Him?

Write it down: set a time and a type of fasting. Let's go!

DAY 5: EVERYDAY REVIVAL: MAKE READY!

A holy desperation for God Himself is what is called for in this hour. Now is not the time to be asking, "God, tell me more about me." Now is the hour to seek all of who God is and let the light of His glory, power, love, mercy, justice, forgiveness, restoration speak to every square inch of our world.

I think by this point in our journey that you and I are ready to rise up and be the church. We won't settle for playing church. And I know we will pray like those who have the ear of the only One who saves—because we do. But first, we know our Higher Pursuit is to seek who God *is* and not just what He offers us. He is the gift. He is the end goal. He is the greatest reward. Jesus changes everything. This is not just a catchphrase to add to our next Instagram post with cute font and a picture of our perfect cup of coffee with our Bible. No, this is a heart cry and desire for everyone in our life to know the only One who brings true mercy, justice, love, grace.

It's a daily prayer: *Holy Spirit, spring forth the wells of revival and awakening. Have Your way. We make ready for You, Jesus!*

Consider the parable Jesus gave in Luke:

> Stay dressed for action and keep your lamps burning, and be like men who are waiting for their master to come home from the wedding feast, so that they may open the door to him at once when he comes and knocks. Blessed are those servants whom the master finds awake when he comes. (Luke 12:35-37)

Be ready. Keep your lamps burning. Keep your passion ignited for Jesus. Live pleasing to Him. Live with His best in mind, knowing that sin is not His best for us. Live knowing you are seen and loved. Let the light of His glory shine through you to overcome the darkness of our world.

We don't know when Jesus will return. But the call here is to be ready with our lives reflecting His glory. Being ready means we are found . . .

- Worshiping no other idol but God Almighty
- Loving our neighbors as ourselves
- Serving our community in the name of Jesus
- Walking in daily repentance
- Feeding on the Word
- Living as one loved (the scarcity mindset has no place in the kingdom of God)
- Offering forgiveness freely
- Doling out mercy in abundance
- Standing for justice, holy justice
- Seeking His face—drawing near because He promises He will be found
- Arming ourselves with the Word, the bread of life
- Grounding ourselves in prayer
- Going low in humility
- Accepting His perfect shalom-peace

- Stepping out in faith

- Gathering heart knowledge of the character of God

- Meeting in deep fellowship with other lovers of Jesus

- Letting the light of His glory shine in and illuminate every square inch of our lives

- Never forgetting Jesus' death on the cross

- Never taking for granted His victory over sin and death. He is risen!

Grab your Bible and journal.

I intentionally kept this chapter short. I would love for you to dog-ear this page to come back to for a pep talk again and again and again.

Let's regroup on the definition of "holy desperation" after you have worked through this chapter and have sat with the scripture included. Write it out. How has it changed since day one?

Take a moment to read the whole parable in Luke 12:35-48. Though we have been instructed to make ready for many, many, many years, there's still a Spirit-led urgency in this passage written so long ago. What does it stir in you?

HIGHER PURSUIT: HOLY DESPERATION

Making ready doesn't make you saved. The holy desperation to go and do, go and tell, sit and adore Him, worship and pray, fast and pray, feed on the Word of life will propel you to make ready out of anticipation and eagerness to partner with the Kingdom. Journal what has kept you more complacent in your walk with the Lord.

Using the "being ready" list above, how will you rise up and be the church today?

CHAPTER 6

HIGHER PURSUIT: FILLED WITH THE SPIRIT

DAY 1: WE DON'T DESIRE NORMAL

I invite you to recall the vision I shared in the introduction: one-dimensional living turned into 3-D fullness in the presence of God. Recall the concept of being off-kilter—trying to make "right" in an effort to get back to normal. I believe many are, in fact, attempting to do just that, yet it's a struggle. The pursuit of what was once "normal" is futile in this day we are in.

To hang onto what once was in an effort to "get back to normal" is to miss where God is moving in what is *now*. The Word of God is full of illustrations, parables, stories reminding us that God is not stagnant. Yes, He often calls us to "be still and know," but that doesn't mean that He isn't moving while He commands us to have a seat and rest in His presence.

Again and again we read the words "rivers of living water" in both the Old and New Testaments. In the next section, we will look at a few of those scriptures. But for now, come back with me to that off-kilter vision. Let yourself be the one-dimensional figure that falls into the river below the cliff. Imagine it's you coming out of the waters full and complete.

Those waters symbolize God's presence. A surrender of your way, plans, agenda then moves you into abundance that comes with God's fullness.

Filled with the Spirit of the living God is where you find yourself because you repented, because you let go of your old ways, your old self.

You declared Jesus as Lord.

You desired His power, love, mercy to inhabit every square inch of your being.

Filled with the Spirit, you are moved to worship Him mind, heart, soul, strength.

She went low (in humility) in surrender to empty herself of "self" agenda and then she rose up to dance in the river of everyday revival. Those rivers of living water sprang forth from her with power, and in His glory, God moved in her and through her.

This is the narrative I want us all to move in as we make the daily, moment-by-moment decision to be *filled with the Spirit*.

Many months after that original off-kilter vision, the Lord gave me more layers to it. It was as if I watched a film and the camera panned out from that one cliff and section of a river in the off-kilter vision. I saw a large span of a canyon with many cliffs and a powerful river twisting and turning through it. At each cliff I saw what can only best be described as a Cirque du Soleil moment with acrobats falling into the water in swan dives. My vantage point was high and wide and I could see the river rolling through as women were not just haphazardly falling into the water from the cliffs but were actively and beautifully diving into the powerful flowing water.

They were actively joining in with the movement of God. He is not stagnant.

What was once a reluctant surrender of an off-kilter feeling and a desire for normal turned into an intentional movement to actively join in on the rivers of living water—God's presence, His active and alive Spirit. They joined in with God and where He was going.

Might this active surrender in beauty and grace be motivated by such scripture as this:

> For this reason I bow my knees before the Father, from whom every family in heaven and on earth is named, that according to the riches of his glory he may grant you to be strengthened with power **through his Spirit** in your inner being, so that Christ may dwell in your hearts through faith—that you, being rooted and grounded in love, may have strength to comprehend with all the saints what is the breadth and length and height and depth, and to know the love of Christ that surpasses knowledge, that you may be filled with all the fullness of God. Now to him who is **able to do far more abundantly than all that we ask or think**, according to the power at work within us, to him be glory in the church and in Christ Jesus throughout all generations, forever and ever. Amen. (Ephesians 3:14-20, emphasis mine)

"Filled with all the fullness of God"—that is what He will do abundantly through the Church. That is what He promises us as individuals though the two can't be separate—the individual and the Church. And He will do just that—more than we could ever wrap our minds around or dream about. The deal with Ephesians 3:20, which is often taken out of context, is that it is not about God fulfilling *our* dreams, hopes, grand plans. It's not about God blowing *our* minds with success. It's about *Him* filling us with His power, love, and understanding of who He is. It's about God filling us abundantly and in overflow with His Spirit. This is all more than our human-limited understanding could comprehend. Isn't that funny—we need the Spirit to understand the depths of this Holy Spirit filling!

Why? We have the divine opportunity to bring glory to God as we join in with the saints of old and with the modern church of Christ too. We get to bring the light of His glory to the ends of the earth and then dive into the rivers of living water—filled to the full. An invitation to refuse stagnation but to join in where God is moving and actively bring restoration and transformation through the gospel to the ends of the earth—this is the abundantly more!

Dive in!

Grab your Bible and journal.

What thoughts do you have after reviewing the off-kilter vision along with the expanded version in today's reading? Does this stir something in you?

Go ahead and take some time to write out Ephesians 3:14-20.

HIGHER PURSUIT: FILLED WITH THE SPIRIT

What does "filled with all the fullness of God" mean?

At this point in our Higher Pursuits journey, where you have actively chosen higher over lesser pursuits, do you see the glorious news that comes with Ephesians 3:20? Do you see the connection of not our goals and dreams being met but abundantly overflowing with God Himself through His Spirit? How does this sit with you right now?

Do you believe you have been filled with the Spirit? We will get into this more in the chapter. Just brain-dump here.

DAY 2: RIVERS OF LIVING WATER

She worked diligently to decorate her family's booth with luscious flowers and fruit. Stringing cherry blossom buds together to drape from the ceiling was her favorite task. Adorning the table with nuts and pomegranates delighted her heart, knowing her family would spend their time together in this sacred space during the Feast of Tabernacles. They worked together to construct the family *sukkah* (booth) with three walls draped of fabric. The roof was constructed from cut branches and leaves. This was all to remember their ancestors in the wilderness after they were delivered from captivity in Egypt. Though the preparation to leave their homes and construct the booth was hard, it was worth it to celebrate God's provision, to thank Him for that season's harvest, to come together and remember the Israelites' 40 years in the wilderness. This was her delight that she looked forward to each year.

As she prepared dinner that evening, she heard a voice that caused her to immediately put down the bowl and spoon to go and listen. She peeked out of the sukkah and something drew her out even more. What was this man saying about living water?

> If anyone thirsts, let him come to me and drink. Whoever believes in me, as the Scripture has said, "Out of his heart will flow rivers of living water." (John 7:37-38)

It was the last day of the Feast of Tabernacles and the priests had just performed their ritual of drawing water from the pool of Silom and pouring it into a silver basin on the altar of the temple. Everyone joined in the prayer on behalf of the nation, asking God to provide heavenly rain for their crops and supply. This ceremony also piqued her excitement for the day in which the Lord would pour out the Holy Spirit. This bold declaration by this unknown-to-her man stirred in her. Did he mean the Spirit of the living God?

> Now this he said about the Spirit, whom those who believed in him were to receive, for as yet the Spirit had not been given, because Jesus was not yet glorified. (John 7:39)

All through the booths, whispers circulated: "Who is this man?" Amongst the skeptics, there were some who carried faith enough to proclaim Him as the Christ—the Messiah. This lit a fire in her heart with anticipation. Was He the one who that wild, rogue prophet-man, John, went on and on about?

> I baptize you with water for repentance, but he who is coming after me is mightier than I, whose sandals I am not worthy to carry. He will baptize you with the Holy Spirit and fire. (Matthew 3:11)

She recalled her time spent watching this baptism of water on the banks of the Jordan River. She came so close to jumping in herself. What kept her? She really didn't know. Was this man outside her booth the one John referred to with such awe and reverence? Wasn't it interesting that he was speaking of living water while John referred to Holy Spirit fire? The common thread: God's Spirit. She heard of it in the Torah stories. That spirit of God she read about hovering over Isreal in the desert and over King David. Would they ever see His Spirit made available to all?

She stepped out of the booth built to remember the One who saves to go and sit at the feet of the One sent to save—one and the same she would soon find out. She wanted the living water *and* the purifying fire. She would repent and be bold to proclaim her faith in the One and with open hands. She would let His rivers of living water flow out of her. Grace. Mercy. Faith. Love. Purity. Power. Righteousness. She wanted to be filled to the brim, to overflow.

If I say it once, I say it a thousand times: Let our hearts' desire be to see the whole earth filled with the knowledge of the glory of God in the face of Christ Jesus, *by the power of the Holy Spirit.*

This book isn't the end-all of higher pursuits; they are, in fact, endless. But these pursuits, carefully selected, serve as a foundation. Also, each intermingle with each other. As this is our final chapter together, let's explore how the pursuit of being filled by the Spirit intertwines with the other pursuits.

Seek His face with awe and reverence, with a biblical worldview, by the power of the Spirit.

This is a lifestyle of choices. True intimacy with the Lord begins by recognizing and understanding *the nature of Himself,* which God poured out in Acts 2 on the day of Pentecost. The Holy Spirit is part of the Trinity: Father, Son, Holy Spirit. Not just an added extra, the Holy Spirit is God Himself dwelling in those surrendered to Christ as Lord and Savior. To fear God, there must be some kind of encounter. Those who are Christ followers are led by the Spirit of wisdom and revelation of the knowledge of who God is. Here is another verse that I will shout from the rooftops: ". . . that the God of our Lord Jesus Christ, the Father of glory, may give you the Spirit of wisdom and of revelation in the knowledge of him" (Ephesians 1:17).

To live with awe, wonder, reverence is to constantly explore God's nature and who He says He is. We do this through His Word and with eyes wide open to creation around us. Through the Spirit, God speaks even in how He flung the moon, sun, and billions of stars into the universe. We are propelled in the journey of revelation by the Spirit. This leads us to deeper intimacy to seek His face. But to set aside the Holy Spirit as an extra add-on in the Trinity is to miss out on the fullness of God. The Holy Spirit gives us insight into God's Word, which then knits us into an understanding of His nature, commands, prophesy. Through the Spirit, our eyes open to see—really see—the grandeur of creation perhaps often taken for granted.

The Holy Spirit is that soft, quiet voice whispering of God's love and mercy right when the good Father knows our soul needs to hear truth. Fear of God and the intimacy of seeking His face can't be separated from the indwelling and daily filling of Holy Spirit.

Pursue holiness and holy desperation, by the power of the Holy Spirit.

The fear of God and the desire for closeness lead to mindsets and actions of holiness. We should please God not for the sake of being a "good Christian gal" but for the sake of honoring God whom we revere and fear. The Holy Spirit equips us with the tools needed for holiness. It's a life that pleases God because we know His best is found within His good boundaries set before us in His Word.

To live desperate for God Himself is to see the world with eyes wide open—*by the power of the Holy Spirit.* The Spirit gives us eyes to see through the lens of the gospel and the desire for Kingdom come. We see what is corrupted by sin but also what *could be* through redemption and restoration—all because of the cross of Christ. Through the Spirit, desperation for God alone propels us to contend and intercede for what could be, should be—what God intended. The Holy Spirit stirs that desire for holiness and desperation for God alone, whose power eclipses the schemes of the devil to pollute and corrupt.

In my studies of revival history, I've seen that revival comes when the presence of God falls on a place or even a region. I've also seen revival fires lit from active repentance of a group or even a nation. This is all because the people involved saw and experienced the Spirit of the living God and couldn't help but repent out of fear and reverence. Where the word "desperate" comes into play is when we read the scripture we've discussed in this section: where Jesus calls those who are thirsty to come to Him and drink living water (see John 7:37-38), rivers of living water—the Holy Spirit. We will discuss John 4 later in this chapter, but in this passage we also see talk of hunger and thirst for living water. Living water: that which is not stagnant but powerful and moving—again, the Holy Spirit. Desperation on the part of the follower of Christ comes in when we come to the end of everything else we think satisfies and only then cry out for God Himself. It's repentance, abundant prayer, worship, more prayer and a desperation for a move of God Himself that are keys to see corporate revival and personal awakening. All of this is propelled by the Spirit of the living God.

There's an important distinction to be made at this juncture. When we surrender our lives to Jesus as Lord and Savior, His Spirit then dwells in us. Baptism of water is a beautiful statement to the world of this decision to live as a Christ follower. But as we've seen in scripture today, Jesus brings a baptism of fire with the Spirit, and the Word commands us to continually be filled with the Spirit. Many believers recognize the Holy Spirit but miss out on the fullness of God offered when we are *continually* filled with the Spirit. That river of living water spoken of by Jesus Himself is a continuous flow, a continual filling. We will dive into this further on day five to add grit and practical ways to live this out. In the meantime, it's important to grasp the value of the Holy Spirit in the Trinity: God the Father, God the Son, God the Holy Spirit—three in one. Separate but still God. All valuable. All three necessary. All three are God.

Isn't it beautiful to sit with this divine mystery of how that is even possible? Isn't the goodness of God so lovely as to offer Himself up on the cross to forgive our sins and to reconcile us back to the original intent? Isn't He so powerful that sin and death—the enemy—were defeated because He rose from the grave? Isn't He so kind to then pour out Himself upon us via His Spirit and dwell within us so that we might further the Kingdom in His power and grace?

Grab your Bible and journal.

With that little bit of context offered regarding the Feast of Tabernacles, read John 7:37-39 again and then write out those verses. This is always a good practice to keep ourselves engaged with Scripture.

Once again, Jesus offers Himself as the ultimate fulfillment of prophesies and practices in the Old Testament. In this scripture, Jesus is declaring Himself as the embodiment of the ritual just performed where the priests placed bowls of water at the altar. He beckons the people to come to Him for provision and sustenance in both body and soul. But Jesus doesn't stop there. He then proclaims that *if* you believe, *then* the living, moving, powerful Spirit of God will flow from you. Not stagnant, stale, old water-sustenance. Flowing water.

HIGHER PURSUITS

What is your heart, soul, mind filled with at this moment? Do you need a refreshing flow of the Spirit of the living God? Why or why not? Journal it out.

Adding the element of the Spirit to our Higher Pursuits, how do you see God's Word and commands as synergistic? Do you see how fear of God is propelled by the Spirit? Do you see the connection between the Holy Spirit and holy desperation, for example? How does this section where we put it all together enrich your desire for Higher Pursuits?

DAY 3: NAME OF GOD: WONDERFUL COUNSELOR

That name, Wonderful Counselor, always takes me back to singing Handel's Messiah: For Unto Us a Child Is Born. I grew up in "high church" with the choir in crisp robes, candles lit, and scratchy panty hose worn by my sister and me under beautiful hand-sewn Christmas dresses my mom designed yearly. My sister and I would pretend we were choir members, making our mouth into big O's like the men and women on stage would do to accentuate the notes and harmonies. With all the joking aside as kids, that amount of reverence given to the Lord in high church formed the awe and wonder I hold today. For that I am grateful.

As I think about being filled with the Spirit as a Higher Pursuit and through our journey of studying the names and character of God, I find it noteworthy that our Wonderful Counselor (the Holy Spirit) is so prominent in this prophetic passage of the Old Testament:

> Hope of all hopes, dream of our dreams,
>   a child is born, sweet-breathed; a son is given to us: a living gift.
> And even now, with tiny features and dewy hair, He is great.
>   The power of leadership, and the weight of authority, will rest on His shoulders.
> His name? His name we'll know in many ways—
>   He will be called Wonderful Counselor, Mighty God,
> Dear Father everlasting, ever-present never-failing,
>   Master of Wholeness, Prince of Peace. (Isaiah 9:6, The Voice)

From the beginning, it was the plan. It was the plan that God would come and annihilate the plans of the enemy through the death and resurrection of the Son—Jesus Christ. God the Father, in His abundant love, so desired His creation reconciled back to Himself that He would send His Son (God Himself—Triune God—three in One) for us. That was always the plan. And as we can see through the words written long before the life, death, and victory of Christ, it was also the plan that God would send Himself poured out like fire and water in the Holy Spirit. Always the plan. Never a reaction or afterthought. Wonderful Counselor is His name. God gave Himself without measure to help us understand *who* the Father is and *how* to live our lives to His delight.

Jesus laid out the plan in Scripture, in the Farewell Discourse. By way of sermons and teachings, Jesus equipped His disciples for life after His death and resurrection. We, too, live on this side of the cross to grab hold of the words spoken of this Wonderful Counselor—Helper promised to come.

Let's add John 14 to Isaiah 9 in our exploration of Wonderful Counselor.

> If you love me, you will keep my commandments. And I will ask the Father, and he will give you another Helper, to be with you forever, even the Spirit of truth, whom the world cannot receive, because it neither sees him nor knows him. You know him, for he dwells with you and will be in you. (John 14:15-17)

Jesus taught them to express love to Him by obeying His commands. But He would not leave them hanging, for a Helper would come to assist in obedience. A Counselor would be poured out to offer wisdom and guidance to live this kingdom-gospel life they would embark upon soon. And what I personally love the most is how Jesus finishes this thought process by offering peace—shalom.

> These things I have spoken to you while I am still with you. But the Helper, the Holy Spirit, whom the Father will send in my name, he will teach you all things and bring to your remembrance all that I have said to you. Peace I leave with you; my peace I give to you. Not as the world gives do I give to you. Let not your hearts be troubled, neither let them be afraid. (John 14:25-27)

Go ahead and grab a pen and mark a line under "my peace I give to you" in this book and in your Bible by way of interacting with the scripture to allow it to live engrained in your mind and heart.

Let's press pause and sit on that. I've mentioned shalom before, but why don't we take a sec to recall a few layers of this word so engrained in the Hebrew language and Jewish culture.

Look above at The Voice translation of Isaiah 9:6; what do you see regarding Jesus as Prince of Peace (shalom)? Wholeness.

Shalom-peace doesn't only mean peace without violence. It has connotations of wellness, blessing, *wholeness*. Now with that in mind, Jesus tells the disciples He will leave them with wholeness. But wholeness of what? Does He mean prosperity or success? No! He means wholeness, fullness of *Himself*. And it gets even better because moments before that, Jesus promised He would send the Helper. We know the Trinity is God, three in One. So let's put this all together:

The Holy Spirit would dwell in believers who surrendered to Christ as Lord and Savior and would be poured out without measure for the goal of offering to them fullness of God Himself.

This begs the need to go deeper in what we need the Wonderful Counselor for exactly. Jesus offers finer details of what this would look like in John 14, in which He also calls it Spirit of Truth. My goodness, don't we presently live in such a day of deception that we need the wind of *the* Spirit of Truth blowing in powerfully? In a time when people hide behind phrases like "well, that's *my* truth," as power-filled, Spirit-filled, world changers who seek higher pursuits, it is our day to seek God Himself and disallow what deceives and blinds in this wild world we live in. This is the time to seek His face like never before. And Jesus discusses that same level of intimacy if you keep reading on into John 15.

> Abide in me, and I in you. As the branch cannot bear fruit by itself, unless it abides in the vine, neither can you, unless you abide in me. I am the vine; you are the branches. Whoever abides in me and I in him, he it is that bears much fruit, for apart from me you can do nothing. (John 15:4-5)

I hope you won't tune out and skim by as I know this verse is super familiar and often quoted. But let's look at God's Word that is alive and active once again in light of the promised Helper. We read in John 14 that Jesus promises the disciples His Spirit, which will actively dwell in them. And then in the same turn, Jesus is talking about abiding in Him. The Spirit dwelling in His followers and His followers abiding in Him—sit with this for a moment. The word "abide" in the original language means dwell, remain, to be held. These words are interchangeable, so what implication does this have on our understanding of the Spirit of the living God promised to us as well?

Initiated by our choice to dwell in Christ, He then gives all of Himself to dwell and abide in us through the Holy Spirit.

This is deep and intimate. It is the source of our true affection and emotion.

We hold His presence like gold. Valuable.

He holds us and keeps us as precious children. Valuable.

The fruit of our lives are the actions, the love, the power, the miracles, the signs, the wonders, the mercy in which God pours out through us—those willing to be continually filled with His Spirit. Valuable.

Because of the Helper dwelling in us, might our fruit be juicy and nutritious to the world around us? Might they, too, taste and see that the Lord is good?!

Grab your Bible and journal.

We covered a lot of ground in John 14 and 15 today. Go ahead and grab your Bible and write out a verse or two that we discussed.

Have you read these passages before? In light of the name of God—Helper, Wonderful Counselor—what new depths in these passages were uncovered for you?

Use these prompts as prayer journaling starters:

- Lord, show me how to remain in You as today I feel a bit far from You...

- Holy Spirit, I need help understanding...

- Forgive me for when I don't value Your presence or allow You to fully dwell in me...

DAY 4: SPIRITUAL DISCIPLINE: IN SPIRIT AND IN TRUTH

By now, I'm hoping that you have grasped the importance of building our spiritual muscles of faith, understanding, prayer, worship, Scripture reading, etc. That word "discipline" can be intimidating as we live in a culture that doesn't value the correction and growth that require a stripping away or a sacrifice of self. But, just as there is goodness to behold in, say, the disciplines of eating healthy whole foods or going to bed to get rest for eight hours, there is glory to behold in buckling up and practicing spiritual disciplines. It's a training ground. This place where we practice and fail, grow and go low, learn and lean into through the power of the Holy Spirit and for the love of our Lord—this place is the training ground to advance the Kingdom in our every square inch.

With that, I admit that today's spiritual discipline is a bit elusive, but will you hang with me? Even if it seems hard to grasp, go ahead and, through grace, do the work to build that muscle of living in spirit and in truth. Work it out day by day. And day by day, the Holy Spirit will lead you to a deeper understanding of the glory of it. I'm believing for you that the Lord will bless your leap into the elusive and unknown.

We will look together at John 4 and the account of Jesus and the Samaritan woman to dive into Spirit and truth. Here in this passage, Jesus is announcing that the followers of God—Elohim—will no longer be required to worship in a temple but have the beautiful freedom to worship wherever they are, wherever their feet take them. Jesus declares that God is Spirit, which proclaims His omnipresence—He is everywhere and will no longer be confined to a temple.

Let's pause for a side note: In this passage, Jesus is ministering with prophetic words, with exhortation, with provision, and with unconditional love to a woman who was thought of in her village as taboo.

Forced to go and collect her daily drinking water in the middle of the day to avoid reproach from the other women, Jesus met her in the heat and in her vulnerability. I will simply drop this thought here: In John 4, Jesus announces that He is the I AM they were all waiting for and He announces the irrelevance of absolute worship in the temple. Jesus declares these profound concepts *all to a sinner and a woman*. If that doesn't speak to your heart and fire you up, I don't know what would!

Will you let the revelation of God's desire to speak to you (yes, you!) propel you to higher pursuits today?

Let's sit on the words straight from Jesus—I AM.

> "But the hour is coming, and is now here, when the true worshipers will worship the Father in spirit and truth, for the Father is seeking such people to worship him. God is spirit, and those who worship him must worship in spirit and truth." The woman said to him, "I know that Messiah is coming (he who is called Christ). When he comes, he will tell us all things." Jesus said to her, "I who speak to you am he." (John 4:23-26)

I can't think of a better example of a life of worship in spirit and in truth, wherever they can be found at any given moment, than in the life of the Chinese Christian Brother Yun. In the book *Heavenly Man*, Brother Yun shares one of the many times he was thrown in prison because of his faith in Jesus Christ. Instead of falling into total despair, Brother Yun saw these times as a divine invitation to move in evangelism and worship within the darkest and dankest of conditions—the wet, smelly, cold cell of a prison. One particular account speaks to my heart: While in prison with fellow Christians who had recently committed their lives to Jesus,

Brother Yun and his brothers opened their hearts to a new inmate who was a violent and hardened criminal. Again, to Brother Yun this was a divine opportunity.

> After Huang [new inmate] received God's salvation, the atmosphere in the cell greatly improved. Everyone began to sing together. Huang was so eager to learn all he could. I taught him about Jesus: His life, teachings, suffering, His resurrection, and the Second Coming.[2]

Before Jesus declared the new era of worship in spirit and in truth wherever people were, the temple was the only place to be in the presence of God Himself. Perhaps people only dedicated their time to worship within the walls of that holy place. These days, I wonder how many Christians check the box and reserve their flat and dispassionate worship to only Sunday mornings? Not us! No, women on a journey of Higher Pursuits know that holy desperation propels them into worship in our cars, in the grocery store line, in our cubicle at work—wherever. I've even spent time with an amazing woman on missions who would bust out her phone in the middle of strip-club ministry and play worship music to shift the atmosphere. Yes, we are called to worship wherever, whenever, because of the Holy Spirit residing in us and offering the profound revelation of who God is. This profound revelation and heart/soul knowledge place us in the mindset that with that knowledge, what else should we possibly do but worship with our life?

Let's not gloss over that Jesus added "and truth" to His bold proclamations to the Samaritan woman. I love the combination of spirit and truth, because on this side of the cross, we need the Spirit to grasp the depth

---

2 Paul Hattaway, The Heavenly Man (Kregel, 2020), 141

and the glory and the beauty of truth. Jesus is truth. He declared Himself in John 14:6 as *the* way, *the* truth, and *the* life and the only way to the Father. Jesus is the fulfillment of Old Testament prophecies and promises that foretold of salvation, reconciliation, and restoration of creation and especially men and women who surrender their lives to Him as the only way. But how do we move in deeper revelation of Jesus as truth?

The Holy Spirit is our Helper to reveal who God is. This Helper, poured out at Pentecost and promised to those who surrender their lives to Jesus, gives us revelation of what God's Word promises. This Wonderful Counselor offers God's utmost wisdom about how to live as salt and light in this world, which seems like it is spinning out. But we don't have to get caught up in the swirl because of the Holy Spirit. This is such comforting news, right?

Our need for truth spills into every square inch of our lives. Might I pose a few examples to get you thinking about many more square inches of your life that need truth?

The world is confusing and corruption, disinformation, division, darkness are rampant.

Know who God is: He is the most just Judge sitting on the ultimate throne.

In spirit and truth: Let the Holy Spirit remind you of hope and shalom—peace in the fullness of God Himself in the midst of the swirl. Let the Holy Spirit offer the truth that God sees and He knows—evil will not win.

Resources are limited and money is tight.

Know who God is: God is the provider, and His kingdom is not about satisfaction in earthly things that fade away but in that which will stand for all of time: love, joy, faith, hope.

In spirit and truth: Let the Holy Spirit overwhelm you with the knowledge of the goodness of God toward you no matter what your bank account says. Let the Holy Spirit drive you to merciful obsession in worship of God instead of the love of things.

Loneliness, comparison, jealousy are real and difficult to manage.

Know who God is: He is the occupier of any void, and He delights to fill you to abundance with His love.

In spirit and truth: Pursue Him with abandon. Let the light of His glory outshine any dark spaces of your heart.

There are many more examples of how living and worshiping in spirit and truth play out in our lives, and we will explore them at the end of this section. But for now, let's dive into what might keep you from living in the fullness of spirit and truth: bitterness. I would love to speak some healing words over you. Even if you don't presently feel the twinge of bitterness, please don't skip this. Many of us have deep roots that need pulling.

Bitter roots are what I see in many these days. Those roots cloud judgment and perspective. Gosh, I know people have hurt you, harmed you, abused you. The Lord weeps when you weep in the pain of trauma to your body, mind, and soul. But please don't translate and equate what a *human* did to harm you in their sin and with an evil heart as an act of God who, in His might and power, loves you tenderly and fiercely.

I'm seeing bitter roots cloud perspective. They offer fertile ground for the enemy of our souls to wreak havoc. I've been there—I know. I've seen bitter roots cause me to spew strings of untruth and hatred. My skin crawls at the thought of how I've let old festering wounds affect how I love others with my actions and words. These bitter roots seem to pop up out of nowhere when I'm in a conversation because something that was said triggered pain. It's time to pull those roots out.

Perhaps bitter roots of pain cause bias and develop clouded judgment of even truth happening in our world right this moment? Might I humbly pitch that out to you right now? Unhealed wounds often leave us blind and vulnerable to those who desire to entrap whole nations in their unbiblical agendas. We see this in history when communists and Marxists saw an opportunity to move in during a volatile time in America when Jim Crow laws raged and ravaged our country. They stepped into very real spaces of pain and injustice and took advantage for their own power play. But the problem is that the wicked agendas remain hidden even all these years later mostly due to blindness and apathy.

This is not a political statement but a warning: wounds and bitterness not submitted before the Lord our Healer lead to either hate-filled acts or simply blindness to the wiles of the enemy of our soul, blindness to how the enemy uses people in wicked and corrupt ways.

My prayer is that we will allow the healing hand of Jesus to dig up the bitter roots in the gardens of our souls. And I know He won't stop there with a void from the uprooted bitterness. Let Him, instead, plant the fruit of the Spirit abundantly: love, joy, peace, patience, kindness, goodness, faithfulness, gentleness, and self-control.

I'm declaring healing and peace over us all in this moment. There is a process to healing, yes. The process is important. And in that process, the bitter roots must be pulled out. The world needs Jesus-loving people operating in clarity (not clouded by very real pain) to see *truth* and to speak His truth to restore what is severely broken around us. Amen? Amen!

Grab your journal and Bible. Let's flesh all of this out.

Where are you today with the spiritual disciplines offered in this book? Do you see them as an opportunity and a training ground? Why or why not? Be honest!

After reading my thoughts and teaching on spirit and truth, read John 4:1-45 and write out a couple of verses to keep yourself engaged with Scripture.

Ask the Holy Spirit to help you understand this discipline of living and worshiping in spirit and truth. What is He showing you?

Take a look at the three examples of how to walk out spirit and truth when life spins out. What personal example would you add to that list? How will you seek to *know who God is* and also operate in *spirit and truth*?

Go ahead and let yourself explore bitterness in your heart and soul. Here are some prayer points to journal and get you started:

- Lord, show me where pain and unhealed wounds are festering...

- Lord, I give You those tender places because I know You are...

- Forgive me for acting in bitterness when I...

- Today I will choose the fruit of the Spirit and I will choose truth...

DAY 5: EVERYDAY REVIVAL: ALL OF HIM WITHOUT MEASURE

"If you then, who are evil, know how to give good gifts to your children, how much more will the heavenly Father give the Holy Spirit to those who ask him!" (Luke 11:13).

I'm a gifts person. As much as I love giving them, I really love getting them! And, my goodness, if my good Father is offering the most glorious gift in the history of time, I want all of it—Him—the Holy Spirit. I want the Holy Spirit for my heart so that I stay true to the knowledge of God's love. I want the Holy Spirit for my mind so that my thoughts align with kingdom principles and revelation in His Word. I want my soul filled with the Holy Spirit so that my emotions and identity are kept in perfect peace—shalom—fullness and confidence in God whom I serve.

If He is pouring it out, I want all of it without measure!

It's as simple as opening the door to my heart, soul, mind. It's all of my heart, soul, and mind because the Father who is the giver of good gifts desires fellowship and to immerse all of me in all of who He is by the power of His Spirit.

But to be honest, this was not always the case. For so long I only had knowledge of and desire for God the Father and God the Son. While this is critical, I was missing that third and equally as critical part of the Trinity, the Holy Spirit. Set to the side as an afterthought, I attempted to do life not in my own strength and without striving as the Bible instructs us. This is a worthy pursuit for sure. But the void in my life was blatant because I was not operating by the power of the Spirit so freely given. "Not by might, nor by power, but by my Spirit, says the Lord of hosts" (Zechariah 4:6).

In my effort to do life and serve the Lord, I also found my self heading around those same old mountains again and again. I confessed constantly of my striving, comparison, jealousy, and so much pride. I repented on the regular. But there was an element missing and it had to do with freedom and power. I was missing what is clearly laid out in the Bible and for all believers: the directive to be filled with the Spirit continually in order to discern and be healed from hurt and pain that perpetuate those old habits and mindsets, those old mountains I couldn't seem to keep from circling. I neglected the Wonderful Counselor, who would help me move into a healthy perspective of life and the shalom-peace-filled ways of living that please the Lord and are good for my soul and spirit.

What is also needed in this hour of history is a level of spiritual discernment like never before. The level of corruption, fallacy, injustice, and straight-up perversion is unfathomable. Yet, even the Church is lulled asleep. Apathy will do that to you. Fear of man will also cause many with a voice and with influence to stay silent for fear of the mob. But not us! Not those of us who seek higher pursuits. We will not fear evil and we will love in the light as Paul instructs in Ephesians 5:8: "... for at one time you were darkness, but now you are light in the Lord. Walk as children of light."

The world seems wild and heavy. It's almost too much to handle when we see clearly the layers upon layers of the enemy's wickedness brought forth these days. But the Wonderful Counselor soothes our souls and continually fills us with the power and the fullness of God Himself. Confidence in the goodness of God and His victory over evil bubbles up to overflowing when we actively live filled with the Spirit of the living God.

Paul continues with a clear directive:

> Look carefully then how you walk, not as unwise but as wise, making the best use of the time, because the days are evil. Therefore do not be foolish, but understand what the will of the Lord is. And do not get drunk with wine, for that is debauchery, but be filled with the Spirit, addressing one another in psalms and hymns and spiritual songs, singing and making melody to the Lord with your heart, giving thanks always and for everything to God the Father in the name of our Lord Jesus Christ, submitting to one another out of reverence for Christ. (Ephesians 5:15-21)

Be wise; don't procrastinate or mess around with your precious time. Don't fill your heart, soul, mind with things that dull your senses and lull you into apathy, for these are things that are lesser pursuits and lesser conversations. We are on the Higher Pursuit journey. Be filled with the Spirit. The original language for the command "to be filled" is not a one-and-done filling. It is a continual pattern to live by.

Here's the good news: we came to this Higher Pursuit of being filled with the Spirit after practicing the other pursuits. Our hearts and minds are already calibrated to forgo the lesser things and seek His fullness!

Let's get gritty with it and put this to practice. Grab your journal and Bible.

Being filled with the Spirit is a constant choice or even a constant course correction to divert our attention from self toward what is spirit and truth. It's a decision to train our thoughts and desires and is propelled by prayer. If you have never been filled with the Holy Spirit, I invite you to pray and even journal out this prayer:

Lord, thank You for pouring out Your Spirit at Pentecost. Thank You, Jesus, for making the way to be in my Father's presence and to be filled with His fullness. I thank You for the cross and resurrection, Jesus. Holy Spirit, I invite You into every square inch of my being. Let Your fire burn deep in me. Let Your living water flow in abundance in me and through me. Give me wisdom and give me revelation of who God is. I want all of You, Lord. Amen!

To be daily filled, to be continuously filled with the Spirit as Paul directs us, I invite you in this prayer on the regular:

Holy Spirit, I choose You today. I quiet my thoughts and I forgo my agenda to align with whatever the Lord wants to do in me and through me today. I surrender with open hands to receive Your power, grace, mercy, love, wisdom, and more. Have Your way, Lord! Amen!

Finally, grab your Bible and journal and read Ephesians 5:1-21. Write out a few verses and then sit quietly, asking the Holy Spirit what He wants to speak to you through this scripture about being filled. Ask Him where you have voids in your life and let Him fill them. Practice His presence by sitting quietly and thinking (meditating) on these verses. Go ahead and leave your phone in another room too. This is how you practically start your day in spirit and in truth!

HIGHER PURSUIT: FILLED WITH THE SPIRIT

Write out what the Holy Spirit has to say.

FINAL THOUGHTS

EXPECTATION VS. ANTICIPATION

There's a level of expectation allowed in the pursuit of everyday revival. I would be remiss if I wrote a book about revival and didn't weave in one of the most commonly quoted scriptures on the topic. Will you take a moment to sit with this verse?

> ... if my people who are called by my name humble themselves, and pray and seek my face and turn from their wicked ways, then I will hear from heaven and will forgive their sin and heal their land. (2 Chronicles 7:14)

Note the words of God: "if my people ... then I will." Because we know who God is and that He keeps His promises, we can expect God to make good on His if/then interaction with the people called by His name. Expectation. Yes. We can expect that God will, in fact, hear our pleas and prayers. We see God make promises in the Old Testament that He fulfills in His perfect way and timing. The most perfect promise was that of the coming Messiah—Jesus. Promises made of old, where generations upon generations longed to behold the Wonderful Counselor, the almighty God, the everlasting Father, the Prince of Peace, invade this dark world with His ever so blinding glorious light.

And on this side of the cross, you and I receive the divine invitation to host God Himself in us as the Holy Spirit moves to guide us in the ways of the Father-God to make Jesus famous in every square inch of our lives. Revival comes when we operate in a holy desperation for God Himself in every square inch of our world—first in us, then through us. That is your call as a woman on a journey of Higher Pursuits: to pray in informed expectation because of your investment of time in His Word and in His presence—expectation coupled with anticipation.

Anticipation leaves room for how God will answer the prayer.

With open hands of anticipation, we take what is expected in Scripture and hold it with open hands. Scripture says God will do immeasurably more:

> Now to him who is able to do far more abundantly than all that we ask or think, according to the power at work within us, to him be glory in the church and in Christ Jesus throughout all generations, forever and ever. Amen. (Ephesians 3:20-21)

We are already familiar with this scripture from previous chapters, but as a reminder, did you know that the main concept of this Insta-worthy Bible quote leads us to expect the Lord will do immeasurably more than we can even fathom regarding saving us from sin, calling us into His loving arms, showing us eternity in His holiness? Let's allow our imaginations to look toward those heavenly, higher pursuits rather than applying this scripture to our earthy pursuits and hopes and dreams and goals, as important as they are to the Lord.

It is up to me to refrain from drawing boundary lines or putting God in a box. My human understanding and limits tempt me to dream only so far in expectation. But by partnering with the Kingdom, I get to await with anticipation for *how* God will bring about revival. The passage in Ephesians reminds us that God's goodness, love, mercy, power are more than we can fathom. His wisdom brings about outcomes where our humanity falls short. But! The Holy Spirit fills in the gap in overflow. Our faith in God's majesty and grandeur places us in a prime position for heavenly anticipation as we await this move of God.

Helpless and hopeless we are not.

It is tempting to sit in disappointment when our timeline doesn't match up with God's. There have been countless times when I've been looking for God's plan to play out, and my nature is to dream and visualize while I plan for myself. I plan and visualize my way into putting God in a box drawn by my own limited human imagination. Gosh, I see ways now that I could have just operated in openhanded anticipation of God's goodness.

Think about the Israelites (God's chosen people) who envisioned their promised land full of milk and honey as something to move into right away. I mean, they did endure centuries of oppression in Egypt! But because of their unbelief that God is who He says He is and that He will do what He says He will do, the original generation of travelers didn't see the promise fulfilled. But Caleb and Joshua went ahead and spied out the land and came back with a report full of anticipation of God's goodness and provision. The rest of the spies cowered at the sight of the seemingly forbidden land full of giants, and reported such. I want to be so quick to bash those unbelieving spies.

Maybe, just maybe, we should look at Caleb and Joshua as Old Testament forerunners of revival. They saw the depth of evil and darkness in front of them yet looked at what could be because of their heavenly anticipation of a move of God to defeat the giants in their God-promised land. Those heaven-oriented boys looked past what *was* and toward how they *knew* God would move—because He said so, because He promised that spacious place for the chosen nation.

Fear and reverence of God will do that. It will move you past boxed expectations and toward heavenly anticipation.

That is where disciplined prayer and worship come in. To be reminded of God's glory, His love, His care of us is to keep worshiping when movement isn't evident.

Revival: an awakening, a renewed awareness of the holiness, glory, power, love of God.

In that awakening we find a place for confession and repentance (the turning away from our sin and toward God's best). Throughout history we see revival prayed for over cities and towns where the glory and presence of God fell like a blanket over the people. Mass repentance broke out with widespread fear of God. Then the tangible presence of God moved people to pray and worship with abandon. Revival has been likened to a fire that spreads over regions and nations because those faithful people yearned and hungered for God Himself—not just for what He could do for them, but for God *Himself*.

Revival only happens because of the gospel. Because Jesus died on the cross and restored our access to fellowship with God the Father, because our sins are paid for, because Jesus conquered death, we can come into the very presence of God—the Creator of the universe and the One who loves us dearly.

EXPECTATION VS. ANTICIPATION

> So let us step boldly to the throne of grace, where we can find mercy and grace to help when we need it most. (Hebrews 4:16)

The gospel truth should awaken our hunger to sit at this throne of grace and never leave. Our life centered at the throne of Jesus motivates us into active prayer and worship in the mundane of our day, in the hard and heavy, and in the ever so good. Now is not the time to sit on the couch of complacent faith, apathy, helplessness, and hopelessness. Rather, when we don't allow the gospel to become routine--when we actively work against taking it for granted--a switch flips in our soul to enlighten us to a bigger Kingdom vision. This is an awakening to God's power, love, and mercy. It ushers in freedom because of Jesus—*freedom from sin and freedom in the fullness of God.* But we can't stop there.

An awakened and renewed state of worship is powerful. We hear accounts in history of people convening for hours and days in prayer and worship because the presence of God fell and covered their midst. I believe that revival in our time looks like the awakening to God's wonder and then a spurring forth to bring His presence and power into schools, offices, gyms, playgrounds, grocery stores. Wherever there are those with eyes to see and hearts humbled to worship Him as Lord, the Holy Spirit will move like fire.

This fire brings boldness to share/speak gospel truth and to love others like Jesus commanded us to do. This fire also brings creativity to live from a place of redemption and restoration--bringing us back to the Creator's original design for humanity before sin changed things. That was the end goal. The death and resurrection of Jesus restore us to what once was when Adam and Eve walked in the cool of the garden in peace and in pure confidence of God's love.

Shalom-peace, renewed awe and wonder, fear, reverence, holy desperation for more—yes, these describe a soul motivated to live in Higher Pursuits and see revival in us and through us.

To finish out our time, let's keep going with what we now know how to do so well—pray!!

Here are some final prayer prompts to get you started:

Holy Spirit, will you continue to fan the flame of my passion for You...

Lord, I surrender my agenda and plans to align with how You are moving in this season. Have Your way...

Thank You, Jesus, for the cross. My gratitude comes from the knowledge that Your death and resurrection changes everything...

Let the whole earth be filled with the knowledge of the glory of God in the face of Christ Jesus, by the power of the Holy Spirit...

EXPECTATION VS. ANTICIPATION

Thank you for joining me in the journey of higher pursuits. God is ever so worthy of our posture of fear and reverence, awe and wonder, intimacy, confession, repentance, valuing His presence, being filled with the Spirit, and more. Keep going higher.

Much love to you,

Sarah

CONNECT WITH SARAH MARTIN

Sarah Martin is a wife, mom, friend, speaker, author, and wanna be artist. Her life mission is to help women create space to see God move in their soul with an invitation to awaken to God's wonder & a vibrant life in His presence. Sarah is the author of the books, **Just RISE UP!** and **Stress Point** and enjoys traveling all over the country to serve women at retreats and conferences. When she is not typing away at her laptop, you can find Sarah on date nights with her husband, shooting hoops with her son, or making a mess in her art room. Read more from Sarah on **Instagram at @sarahfmartin**

WITH GRATITUDE

I'm ever so grateful for my supportive husband Greg and son, Grayson. The hours that I sneak away to write only to come back to a clean house is ministry in itself. Thank you.

Thank you to my dear friend, Joan Quintana, for doing a theological review on Higher Pursuits. Your life as a whole inspires me and there is no one else I would have trusted more with this manuscript than you!

Thank you to Julie and Paul Fowler. Your mentorship and support makes this thing I do feel less lonely.

Thank you to Larry Sparks, my revival mentor. I have devoured your content online and in books and I'm grateful for your teaching that calls me into these Higher Pursuits.

Made in the USA
Middletown, DE
28 January 2024